TRAVEL FORWARD

This edition published by Highpoint Life.

For information, write to info@highpointpubs.com.

First Edition

ISBN: 978-0-9891054-6-0

Library of Congress Cataloging-in-Publication Data

Murphy, Mark

Travel Forward

Summary: "Travel is not just about getting on a plane and jetting off to some foreign locale. Even when we are close to home, we can generate a positive force to make a huge difference in the quality of our lives. Nationally recognized travel expert Mark Murphy offers inspirational observations, essays and exercises that enable the reader to Travel Forward."—Provided by publisher.

ISBN: 978-0-9891054-6-0 (hardbound)

1. Self-Help 2. Motivational

Library of Congress Control Number: 2013950601

Design by Sarah Clarehart

10 9 8 7 6 5 4 3 2 1

Travel Forward

MARK MURPHY>

> Contents

Travel Forward

"It's not the mountain we conquer, but ourselves."
—Sir Edmund Hillary

"Twenty years from now you will be more disappointed by the things you didn't do than by the ones you did do. So throw off the bowlines, sail away from the safe harbor. Catch the trade winds in your sails. Explore. Dream. Discover."
—Mark Twain

"One's destination is never a place, but a new way of seeing things."
—Henry Miller

"I am prepared to go anywhere, provided it is forward."
—David Livingstone

Where do you want to go in the world, in life?

Travel is a powerful concept. It's not just about getting on a plane and jetting off to some foreign locale. Even when we are close to home, we can generate a positive force to move ourselves forward.

You know when you hit that sweet spot. It happens at different times, and in different ways, but the feeling is unmistakable. At the most basic level, it's a feeling of energy that washes over you and puts you into a positive state of mind. Taken further, it is the serenity and vitality that characterizes a life filled with positive, conscious choices.

Maybe you held open a door for someone and, instead of a mumbled "thanks," he looked you in the eye and really meant what he said. Perhaps you were in a rush on the highway but eased up to let someone over in front of you—and she waved. You felt those moments.

That special feeling might have happened the day you decided to ignore the voice in your head that kept saying, "It's too late to make that change," and you took on a huge risk, one step at a time. It might have occurred when connecting with an ailing loved one, or taking in a stunning mountain vista, when you understood that "right now" is all there is.

It doesn't matter whether the situation, the moment, is small or large. The feeling—that unmistakable positive charge—is the same.

This feeling becomes far more profound when you get outside of your local culture and customs and experience the world. It can't be understood or appreciated by some book, even this one, or a television show or Hollywood movie. It has to be *experienced*. That experience is something that you as an individual must undertake. Indeed, it's about you, and the people you've never even met. One thing is true: we are all connected at our most basic level, and that connection is the world we all share.

Personal observation and experiences, at their root level, will help you capture the essence of a people a place and ultimately, a feeling. If you want to get the most out of this book, and this movement, then you need to see the world, one step at a time. Creating positive feelings are just the beginning.

It can all start with a wave and a smile. Simple gestures set the course for our travels and become the constant fuel that carries us along. Each of them marks another mile in the journey to our destination in life. By acting with positivity in these moments, we move ourselves, and those around us, forward. We come to a crossroads, we make a connection and the magic of Travel Forward grabs us.

TRAVEL FORWARD DESTINATIONS

Jot down your thoughts about destinations and what they mean to you. There are physical world destinations, such as the Canadian Rockies, the Great Barrier Reef, Mesa Verde or the Sistine Chapel. What are your favorites? Why do you find them compelling?

There are also personal destinations—places you may want to take yourself as a person, a father or mother, a teacher or a friend. Which ones do you aspire to? What would arriving at these inner places mean to you?

Write your answers here now. We'll come back to them at the end of the book.

THE PHYSICAL WORLD

Destination	Why it reflects your values
Canadian Rockies	Striving for goals; spiritual purity
St. Lucia	Living in the moment

YOUR PERSONAL WORLD

Destination	Why it reflects your values
Regular, dedicated volunteer	Helping others; making world better
Smiling more at strangers	Spreading happiness; promoting oneness

What Are the Keys to Happiness?

The stories in this book reflect the core values embodied in Travel Forward moments. When one of these moments happens to you, life is giving you a gift—one that you can use to Travel Forward. Here's how I see the core values embodied by these moments:

- **INTEGRITY:** Do the RIGHT thing. REACH out to others.
- **LOVE:** Show your GRATITUDE. HUG, HOLD and CHERISH those around you.
- **LIFETIME OF LEARNING:** Bring childlike CURIOSITY to everything you do.
- **SELF-DETERMINATION:** Reach your GOALS. You CAN do it!
- **ONENESS:** Create CONNECTIONS and RECOGNIZE what makes us all alike.

Each Travel Forward moment gives you a model for living. They're happening everywhere, all the time. You just need to open your eyes to see them!

"Unexpected
intrusions of
beauty. This is
what life is."

—Saul Bellows

Integrity

> " Without courage, we cannot practice any other virtue with consistency. We can't be kind, true, merciful, generous, or honest."
> **—Maya Angelou**

"True forgiveness is when you say 'thank you for that experience.'"

—Oprah Winfrey

The Power of Forgiveness

Anger and bitterness towards someone who wronged you is a natural feeling that many of us share at one time or another. We think about revenge in many cases, and even plot to exact it. We don't let go.

By not letting go we allow negative feelings to grip and control us. Those feelings put down roots, become deeper and cause us to grow even more hostile. They affect our health and well-being, not to mention our relationships moving forward.

Imagine being held prisoner in an island fortress and serving hard labor for believing in equality. You spend 27 years of your life in an isolated and harsh environment, finally getting released when you are an old man. It would be easy to be bitter and spend your remaining years wallowing in self-pity and anger. Indeed, nobody would blame you if you did exactly that.

But someone did suffer this exact fate, and yet he emerged to embrace an entire nation and complete a movement that began decades earlier. This is the story of **Nelson Mandela,** who many believe was the single driving force behind the end of apartheid in South Africa.

How can one person seemingly let go of something so traumatic while another hangs onto the deep bitterness that grows from injustice? What's different about that one person versus the other? In some cases it comes down to what each chooses to focus on.

Did Nelson Mandela focus on his own troubles during those years of imprisonment, or did he contemplate the larger cause for which he was fighting? Most would say he focused on everything but himself during that horrific time, never veering from his goal of freeing his people from a government that made them second-class citizens.

Anyone who has ever traveled to South Africa has seen the segregated shantytowns where many of the blacks and the coloreds, as the white government described them, were forced to live. Did those images stay with Mandela during all of those years in prison? Did they create a determination that allowed him to overcome the individual wrongs that were committed against him? Did those same images drive him, even in captivity, to ultimately correct the wrongs of an entire country?

We can take how Nelson Mandela handled the most extreme of ordeals and apply it to our lives when we experience an injustice. We may question ourselves and ask if we really can "turn the other cheek." Of course we can, as evidenced in Mandela, but it's up to each of us to **discover forgiveness within our own hearts.**

Embracing forgiveness for a perceived wrong is an act of traveling forward.

When you believe in a cause, as Mandela did, it is bigger than anything that can happen to you as an individual, with geometrically more potential to change your behavior and potential for fulfillment. For many, this is the root driver of their ability to look beyond their own personal situation and towards a greater purpose or goal. Bitterness and resentment stand in the way of that purpose. By casting aside those feelings, and embracing forgiveness, you free yourself to Travel Forward in life. ■

TRAVEL FORWARD

Think about forgiveness. If you hold onto anger, it will eat away at you. If you isolate that anger in a mental box, and forgive someone who may have wronged you, you will be set free.

▶ Write down two "wrongs" that have been perpetrated on you by others:

1 ....
....
....
....

2 ....
....
....
....

▶ Why hold those in your heart when they only hurt you? Make a commitment today to Travel Forward by letting them go. Take an action that symbolizes your forgiveness and freedom from this weight.

....
....
....
....
....
....

6

"When another person makes you suffer, it is because he suffers deeply within himself, and his suffering is spilling over. He does not need punishment; he needs help. That's the message he is sending."

—Thich Nhat Hanh

What is a

CAUSE THAT YOU BELIEVE IN

—one that you think would transcend any suffering

you would absorb from the hands of others?

Describe your cause and share why it would help

you forgive by posting anywhere using **#TravelForward.**

View the film *Invictus*,

starring **Morgan Freeman** and **Matt Damon**. It is the inspirational story of Nelson Mandela's ability to forgive and the gifts it brought to his country. Watch the **trailer** online now.

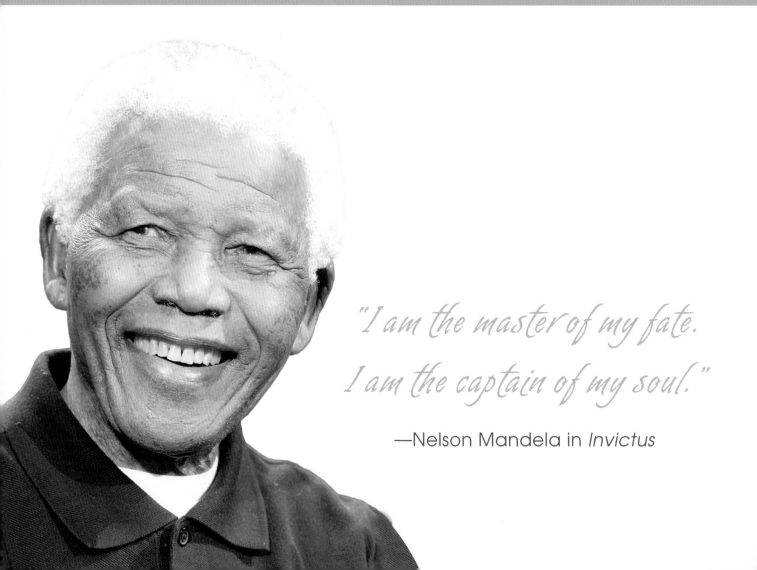

"I am the master of my fate. I am the captain of my soul."

—Nelson Mandela in *Invictus*

"If you don't like the way the world is, change it. You have an obligation to change it. You just do it one step, at a time."

—Marian Wright Edelman

From Small Steps ...

Great things come from small steps. You just have to start walking—traveling forward. You don't need to know your ultimate destination or even have an arrival time. In fact, you'll probably never arrive in the traditional sense, and that shouldn't bother you.

Time and time again, individuals have taken those small steps, powered by their creative ideas and their own sense of integrity. These folks weren't trying to change the entire world all at once but just started moving in the direction in which they felt driven. Their inspiration has made a difference and continues to grow, changing for the better the lives of thousands.

Linda and Willard Fuller's Habitat for Humanity

Take, for example, Habitat for Humanity (www.habitat. org). The idea for this organization emerged in 1968, when a Christian farm community in Georgia set aside 42 lots for families in need. The idea was to raise capital and use volunteers to build the houses at no profit, and no interest cost, to the families.

Linda and Willard Fuller were involved in this group and ultimately took the idea to Zaire in 1973. There they focused on creating 2,000 affordable homes for those who needed them the most, dedicating three years of their lives to the effort. After returning to the United States in 1976, the Fullers formed what has become the Habitat for Humanity we all know today. From humble beginnings and a single idea, this organization has moved on to far larger endeavors and results, one house at a time. By 2013, this organization had either repaired or built more than 600,000 homes for more than three million people throughout the world.

Jon Bon Jovi's Soul Kitchen

Jon Bon Jovi is known for his music but not necessarily for his side job. Motivated to fight poverty and homelessness, in 2004 he became an owner of the Philadelphia Soul arena football team, part of the nonprofit Philadelphia Soul Charitable Foundation, which was dedicated to helping the lives of those in need. In 2006, this group became the Jon Bon Jovi Soul Foundation, with Bon Jovi himself acting as board chairman.

Through his organization, Jon Bon Jovi has raised millions of dollars and helped bring people back from the precipice of economic despair. In 2011, he launched the Soul Kitchen (www.jbjsoulkitchen.org), a unique restaurant in Red Bank, New Jersey, which has no prices on the menu. You simply pay what you want towards your meal, or enjoy a meal at no cost or volunteer as staff if you don't have the means to pay. Diners sometimes ask what they should pay and are told that $10 covers the basics of any given meal, with additional dollars going towards feeding someone else.

It's not a complicated concept, and it's only in a single location, but it's working for the Red Bank community. Those who can pay a little more do it while helping their neighbors who can't. The feelings fostered on all sides are hard to explain, but you know it when you feel it. By dining there, and contributing to your meal, you are making a difference.

> **"Take the first step in faith. You don't have to see the whole staircase, just take the first step."**
> **—Martin Luther King, Jr.**

This restaurant could have been founded as a traditional soup kitchen where the only people who go there are the ones who are down on their luck. Instead, it opened its doors to anyone interested in great local food, whether they have money or don't.

Both the Fullers and Bon Jovi volunteered their time and energy to bring along those less fortunate in the process. This has led others to follow them as they become empowered to create change, one step at a time. In the case of the Soul Kitchen, those initial steps might lead to a meal earned and the pride that goes along with the experience. In both cases, these individuals helped to empower communities to come together for their neighbors.

Habitat for Humanity's community has expanded all over the globe in the five-plus decades since its formation, while the Soul Kitchen is just underway. Starting with small steps can lead to big things. The key is to get walking and Travel Forward. ■

TRAVEL FORWARD

Habitat for Humanity and Jon Bon Jovi's **Soul Kitchen** are just two of many entrepreneurial efforts that are continuing to better our world. Some other notable startups include:

* **The Brooklyn Grange** (www.brooklyngrangefarm.com) is a 40,000-square-foot commercial organic farm located on the rooftops of New York City. It sells fresh vegetables to local residents while providing job opportunities through urban farming.

* **Lava Mae** (www.lavamae.org), a San Francisco nonprofit, converts old city busses into portable showers and toilets that can provide services to up to 130 homeless residents each day.

* **Lufa Farms** (www.lufa.com), located in Montreal, bills itself as the first commercial rooftop greenhouse in the world. At 31,000 square feet of growing space, it produces fresh vegetables year-round and offers a membership system where people can pick up same-day-picked produce at specified locations.

All of these businesses were started by creative individuals with a big idea and the desire to do good things.

SO LOOK AROUND ...

1. What local businesses in your area are improving the fabric of society through innovation?

2. Now **do some research.** What do the histories of these businesses tell you about their founders? Break down their success stories to the single steps they took to build their ventures. Can you follow in their footsteps?

Spread the word about these businesses, and others which you may be connected via social media **#TravelForward.**

Putting It Out There ...

Sixto Diaz Rodriguez is a modern-day Cinderella or maybe some kind of Buddhist monk. Like Nelson Mandela, this man played a role in the South African revolution without ever leaving his neighborhood in Detroit.

Rodriguez is a 70-year-old American folk-rock musician who, in his younger years, performed in the mold of Bob Dylan. He cut a couple of albums, *Cold Fact* and *Coming from Reality*, in the early 1970s. They garnered some critical kudos, but this guy apparently had lousy management; his records bombed and his career never went anywhere—or so he thought.

After his albums tanked back in the day, Rodriguez gave up the music business, put down his beat-up guitar and went back to the construction jobs that sustained him in his native Detroit. He raised a family and worked at some of the toughest jobs in the construction business: demolishing rooms, hauling debris and the like.

But here's the thing: While Rodriguez was living his hardscrabble life in anonymity, his records turned up in South Africa and were passed around from person to person. His Dylanesque tunes about justice and freedom struck a deep cord among those fighting for the abolition of apartheid in their country. Even though nobody over there knew who this guy really was, his popularity exploded as the fight for freedom and equality came to a head. Rodriguez became a national star in South

"Art must take reality by surprise."

—Françoise Sagan

Africa, selling millions of records, while his songs became, quite literally, the soundtrack for the revolution.

In the meantime, back in Detroit, Rodriguez was oblivious. In fact, he didn't find out about his amazing success in South Africa until a few years ago. That's when Swedish-British filmmaker Malik Bendjelloul began working on his documentary, *Searching for Sugar Man*, which followed two Cape Town fans in the late 1990s as they pursued their quest to discover if the rumored demise of this mysterious American star was really true. The film became a huge international hit, ultimately winning the 2012 Academy Award for "Best Documentary."

Rodriguez has now attained global recognition, more than four decades after his two albums were recorded. He is touring the world and appearing on television—all while continuing to live in the low-income Detroit apartment building where he has spent his entire adult life. He's now making a lot of money from album sales and touring, but you'd never know it from his humble lifestyle. He loves performing but apparently has little interest in financial riches or material possessions. You could say that he has more in common with a monk than with the pop star who helped drive one of the 20th century's most notable human rights movements.

Here's a person who **humbly put out his gift into the world** and, with no further effort or guidance, his artistic effort was key to ensuring freedom for millions of people. The U.S. marketplace had told him that his musical skills were all but worthless—that he had nothing to offer—but look what happened! Without regard to what other people might think of him, and without any real profit motivation, Rodriguez just did what came naturally.

Every one of us has a gift to bring to the world, and we should never be afraid to express ourselves, no matter what someone might try to tell us. Follow your muse, put your special gift out there and something good (maybe even great) may happen. You're likely to brighten some lives—somewhere and some time—whether you find out about it or not! ∎

TRAVEL FORWARD

If you were to pick five things that you would like to explore outside of your current life's endeavors, what would they be? Place these in order of priority. Imagine how it would feel to learn and experience even a hint of all those things. Think about how any of these might make a positive difference to others.

1 _____

2 _____

3 _____

4 _____

5 _____

Now get started—even a tiny bit—with #1. You have a whole year to explore it.

Tell us where you want to travel in life and get your fellow travelers' feedback and encouragement #TravelForward.

"By leaving your comfort zone behind and taking a leap of faith into something new, you find out who you are truly capable of becoming."

—Unknown

20

GET INSPIRED!

If you haven't yet seen *Searching for Sugar Man*, watch the trailer and then rent the film!

SEARCHING FOR SUGAR MAN

Compassion Brings Headaches ...

Football is a violent sport. Anybody who has ever played the game knows this truism. But, unlike other sports where it might not be as apparent, everybody watching the game understands the violence as they inevitably see players go down and, in some cases, not get up on their own.

The rules of compassion don't apply on the field, or so it appears, as players must make and take the hits that leave their bodies damaged beyond repair. Knock a player out of a game, and you might be rewarded with some extra cash or what's known as a "bounty." As we have learned, in the 2009-2010 season, the New Orleans Saints leadership apparently did just that. Players on the opposing team were targeted, and any Saints player who could take them out of the game would be rewarded. The ultimate goal was to win, period. If taking somebody out of play could make that easier, then so be it.

In 1989, during a Colts/Jets football game, **Freeman McNeil,** a running back for the Jets, laid a block on O'Brien Alston, the Colts linebacker, shredding his knee. From reports on the field, a sickening crack could be heard as Alston went down, and he was eventually carted off the field. For 10 minutes, McNeil barely moved from the sideline where he knelt. It was evident that he was deeply impacted by the injury and appeared to be in a funk. That funk would continue for most of the game in which he apparently missed assignments, carried the ball only two times in the second half and ultimately caused the Jets to lose.

According to an article in *Sports Illustrated*, McNeil was so distraught after the game that he approached Alston, who was outside his locker room on crutches, with tears in his eyes. He apologized for the damaging hit, and Alston replied, "These things happen."

> "The key to developing compassion in your life is to make it a daily practice."
>
> —Leo Babauta

The head coach of the Jets, Joe Walton, had this to say: "I've never seen anything like it. I understand his feeling, but that's the way the game goes. Obviously, it [allowing his remorse to affect his play] was not a good thing ... and he realizes that."

Should a football player show any remorse when his action causes severe injury, especially when it's unintentional? Should human feelings be left in the locker room because you might not be able to play your best? I couldn't disagree more.

As human beings, we have a connection to each other that is sometimes hard to see in the heat of competition. Coaches invoke phrases like, "We are going to war ...," and refer to areas on the field as the "trenches," akin to the long ditches that were dug in the battles of World War I. They talk about the "fight" or the "battle" to take place so much that you, as a player, are in a "battle mindset" versus an "athletic competition."

These references are part of the strategy to fire up players and get them to give their all. By emphasizing the fact that competition is more than a game, coaches can get players to dig more deeply than they might have thought possible. Critically important, however, is knowing when to drop to your knee with the understanding that it's not a war by any stretch; in the end, it's simply a game.

The pressure of that day and the will to win led to Freeman McNeil later apologizing for letting his team down. Instead of accepting a moment where his true feelings were exposed for all to see, he pulled back into himself and the game of football. He buried the moment.

I never have spoken to Freeman McNeil, but I'd be interested to know if his view has changed now that he is many seasons removed from the game. If he were addressing young kids getting ready to play in a game, would he conjure up a battle cry or reach for his common humanity?

When someone falls in a competition, there isn't any shame in showing what is inside all of us: the heart of a human being that knows it's more important to be remorseful and show compassion than to just put a win on the board. To my mind, that's a core component of integrity.

When we show that heart, we all win. In doing so, we Travel Forward. ∎

TRAVEL FORWARD

There's no doubt: **Compassion will nourish your spirit,** giving you the happiness and energy you need to do great things. Try integrating these practices into your everyday life.

When you wake up each morning, think about the following: "Today I am fortunate to have woken up. I am alive. I have a precious human life. I am not going to waste it. I am going to use all my energies to develop myself, to expand my heart out to others."

At the family dinner table, make a point to find out what others have accomplished that day, what victories were achieved and what honors or "good things" they received. Then, take at least 10 minutes to commend those who have had good days, making a "fuss" over them and experiencing their joy. (Thanks to the Rev. James Forbes.)

Think of people you know who have shown compassion and list them on the next page. Think of the ways they inspire you and how you can follow their example.

These Folks Inspire Me.

Who   How they showed
                                       compassion to others

1 ....

2 ....

3 ....

4 ....

5 ....

List three ways in which you have shown compassion to others during the past week. Write down three new things every week.

1 ....
....

2 ....
....

3 ....
....

Share your compassion stories. **#TravelForward.**

Independence for All

A young man or woman feels the call to serve. They join the armed services and begin a path that is supposed to lead them to a better life. They survive boot camp, training missions and ultimately their first deployment. Most members of the armed services ultimately return to the civilian world with experiences in leadership and overcoming obstacles that only come with this choice. Their lives get back on track with their families and other friends. Regardless of what they may have seen and experienced in combat, they come back to a world that is the epitome of "normal." Most are able to step back into their old lives, and build new ones, after their time on duty.

For others, the road back is far more challenging. They may have lost limbs or their eyesight—or both. Twenty percent of the soldiers who have deployed to Iraq and Afghanistan are affected by post-traumatic stress disorder, which is more than 300,000 suffering from injuries that aren't visible to the casual observer. These folks struggle each and every day to overcome their injuries in the

"Start where you are. Use what you have. Do what you can."

—Arthur Ashe

> **"Ultimately these aren't just causes—they're human beings who need our help."**

—Ben Affleck

face of challenging hurdles and setbacks. Groups like the **Wounded Warrior Project (WWP)** (www. woundedwarriorproject.org) raise money to help wounded veterans get their lives on track. They host events and provide other services to these veterans and their families as they begin the long task of rebuilding from the inside out. Some of these people may never get their eyesight back, or be able to walk, but they are indeed succeeding and even thriving with the help of their families and these groups.

I was recently watching a Fox News broadcast of *The O'Reilly Factor.* On this particular segment, **Bill O'Reilly** showed a product called the "Track Chair," a veritable all-terrain wheelchair that was designed to provide the independence that can't be realized in traditional models. An organization called **The Independence Fund** (www.independencefund.org/) wanted to raise enough money to provide 1,700 of these personal vehicles to our wounded soldiers.

Thanks to the media exposure that O'Reilly provided, many of these people are well on their way to regaining their independence as they Travel Forward from their horrific injuries. In just a few short months, and with little more than O'Reilly's words, The Independence Fund had received more than $8 million in donations.

Through his television show, O'Reilly has the ability to reach and influence millions of people each and every day, and has raised large sums of money for charities such as the WWP and The Independence Fund. (His reminders of the sacrifices made by our veterans encouraged my family to donate to the WWP, and we've consistently given over the years to this worthwhile organization.) By simply reminding people of the sacrifices that our service members make, O'Reilly inspires us to sacrifice where we can. He particularly asks companies and wealthy individuals to support these great causes, and many have answered the call. This effort by everyone involved is a great example of patriotism.

"In the very act of giving, I experience my strength, my wealth, my power. This experience of heightened vitality and potency fills me with joy."—Erich Fromm

O'Reilly is a conservative, but it doesn't matter what side of the aisle you are on when it comes to these kinds of causes. Regardless of your political leanings, you have to admire when someone in a position of power and influence encourages people to Travel Forward and help others. The regular updates I receive have shown that The Independence Fund is getting ever closer to their goal of 1,700 Track Chairs for wounded vets. That's a remarkable feat, which is only possible when those with a megaphone get out there and use it.

So how can you make a difference if you're not a television personality or a pop star? Today, we all have our very own megaphones. They are called Facebook, Twitter, Pinterest—name your favorite social media. By utilizing these platforms to share information on groups like The Independence Fund, **you can express your love and concern** to the members of our society who need our assistance, deepening your own happiness in the process. You can make a collective impact that far exceeds the reach of even Fox News, CNN or the major broadcast networks. This is a relatively new phenomenon that is changing the world and, when applied to positive initiatives like these, it dramatically improves the lives of our veterans.

Here's a final thought on The Independence Fund and its approach to raising money: Nearly every dollar the organization raises goes toward the veterans they are helping with Track Chairs and other programs. Nobody in the charity takes a salary, and they spend no money on advertising. It all happens because of people like them, and people like you, who understand that we are all in this together. ■

TRAVEL FORWARD

Helping others is important and a responsibility that we all have, but just as notable is the unequaled joy and fulfillment that giving brings. **Think about the ways you have given,** both large and small. In what ways did these acts make you feel good? Did that feeling of fulfillment help you accomplish anything else—for yourself or for others? Think about it, and jot your thoughts here.

Ways I have given	The positive effect on me
1	
2	
3	
4	
5	

The Social Media Megaphone

Are you on Facebook, Twitter or a similar social network? Have you ever used Kickstarter (www.kickstarter.com) or Indiegogo (www.indiegogo.com) to raise funds? Have you ever taken part in a runathon or biking event to raise pledges? Jot down some ideas about how you can help your favorite causes (or friends in need) by promoting them on social media, whether through links, fundraising, concerts or other creative forms of promotion.

1 ....
....

2 ....
....

3 ....
....

Now share these ideas via **#TravelForward.** Find out what others are doing and how to connect with their special projects! Synergy is a powerful thing, so don't hesitate to jump in!

The Most Important Journey

He loved to cycle. Indeed, he had a passion for it and told me how he had traveled from Seattle to Boston in a single journey spread over many weeks. He spent time in France, cycling across that country as well. On his greatest trip ever, he set off from Prudhoe Bay, Alaska, with the intent on cycling to the bottom of South America, and doing it in world record-setting fashion.

I learned this on a flight from Chicago to Aspen as I was en route to catch up to my family for a spring break snowboarding vacation. The person telling me this was **Wayne Ross,** one of a group of disabled veterans who had taken over half of the airplane. These guys were on their way to the National Disabled Veterans Winter Sports Clinic, an event designed to give them the opportunity to learn how to ski, drive a snowmobile and more—despite their injuries.

I first noticed this group at the gate, where there were more wheelchairs lined up than I had ever seen for any single departure. The fact that the flight was going to Aspen, the winter playground of the rich and famous, made it seem all the more odd. I initially wondered what these people would do in Aspen but, when I asked a uniformed military member standing nearby, I found out in a hurry.

"We make a living by what we get; we make a life by what we give."

—Sir Winston Churchill

35

The sight of so many wounded warriors at the gate was a reminder of the incredible sacrifices that they have made for our country. Many had been injured in the line of duty, and their prosthetics and wheelchairs made it clear that their sacrifices were more than most of us could imagine. It felt both disturbing and disheartening to initially see the state of many of these travelers. That feeling didn't last, as they would never let you feel sorry for them or their situation. Indeed, in several conversations aboard the flight, I felt their amazing energy and determination.

Wayne Ross was just such a guy, and he shared his story with me. In the 1990s, his friend's father was suffering from multiple sclerosis. He set out on his bike to raise money as part of what he hoped would be a record-setting event. Instead of making it all the way to the bottom of South America, his journey ended in Guatemala City. A head-on collision with a bus caused a broken neck and left him as a quadriplegic for life.

In a desire to raise money and awareness for people suffering from a crippling disease, Wayne's ride took him instantly to a place where many multiple sclerosis sufferers end up: in a wheelchair.

The irony wasn't lost on me as I learned his story. Had people stepped up to repay that favor to him now that he was in a tough situation? Did his ability to pay it forward—or Travel Forward—when he was healthy come

"Every single one of us has a good work to do in life. This good work not only accomplishes something needed in the world but completes something in us."—Flannery O'Connor

back to him as injuries impacted his life? Those questions never had a chance to be asked and became less and less relevant as the flight wore on.

As we spoke further, I could see that Wayne was in a different place than many who may have suffered something similar. His focus wasn't on himself but on the veterans on that plane and the upcoming event.

As it turns out, Wayne is involved in supporting the event as a volunteer and not just a participant. Many years ago, his life changed forever when the bicycle he was traveling on crossed paths with a Guatemala City bus. I didn't see or hear any regret as he recounted the story of how he ended up in his situation. I only noticed an innate **integrity and determination** to continue his journey on two wheels, via a different mode of transportation. This particular journey would take him forward as he traveled to Aspen. ■

TRAVEL FORWARD

Sometimes a personal experience is what we need to mobilize us and give us the empathic energy to help others on a larger scale. Are you or have you been involved in any group efforts to help people in need? What life events drew you to this work?

Think of several people or causes that have helped or inspired you. What are some ways that you can "pay it forward" and help out these particular groups?

Personal inspiration	How I paid/will pay it forward
1	
2	
3	

In Iroquois society, leaders are encouraged to remember seven generations in the past and consider seven generations in the future when making decisions that affect the people. There are lessons here for looking at life.

Wayne's spirit and commitment helps us remember that what's most important is to be there for each other, and to treasure each moment we have in life, regardless of our circumstances. What is one thing that you can do to help someone (and possibly change the world) in the next week?

1

Share your stories of dedication, compassion and paying it forward using #TravelForward. I may pick yours for my next book!

"A life lived for others is the only life worth living."

—Albert Einstein

Love and Gratitude

2

> " We can only be said to be alive in those moments when our hearts are conscious of our treasures."
> **—Thornton Wilder**

"**Life** is what happens when you're busy making other **plans**."

—**John Lennon**

The Diagnosis

It was a sunny Friday evening in a quiet suburb north of New York City. A couple sat in their backyard and watched as their six-month-old son bounced up and down in a jumper, making noises and bringing a smile to their faces.

His chubby cheeks, bright red hair and big blue eyes brought joy to both parents as they stared in amazement at what they had created. They had recently purchased their first house, in anticipation of the little bundle that would soon grace them both. It was a small house in a beautiful town, but it had plenty of space to accommodate their family and even a visitor on occasion.

The backyard ran straight out from the rear patio and ended at a fieldstone wall that dated from a bygone era. A light breeze carried the sweet smell of fresh flowers as the leaves gently swayed in their tree-lined, picture-perfect yard. As the couple alternated their gaze from their son to the beautiful setting, they both felt a sense of contentment that neither had ever experienced before. Life was good; indeed, life was damn good.

It was 1997 and this small family was just taking shape: the house in the suburbs, a good job in the city and a beautiful town to begin raising the first of what they hoped to be many children.

A few months earlier, on a follow-up visit to her obstetrician, the wife mentioned numbness in her left arm. Her doctor examined her and told her not to worry, mentioning that it could be an after-effect related to the birth, or simply a byproduct of hauling around a 10-pound, very round package of love. He told her to let him know if the symptoms persisted or if, as he seemed to expect, they might simply fade away. At this point, their son had just hit two months of age.

Thirty days passed and, with nothing changed, the doctor referred the wife to a neurologist. The doctor performed a number of seemingly meaningless physical tests, sharing nothing in the process. A few weeks and a few tests later, he suggested a spinal tap in order to examine her spinal fluid and either eliminate or confirm his potential diagnosis.

The test came and went, and they returned to their normal schedule, ending up in the backyard on that beautiful summer night. The ringing of the phone interrupted the evening, and the young mother jumped up to answer it. It was the doctor calling.

He asked if her husband could join them on the call and, with the phone balanced between their two heads, and standing just a few feet from their newborn baby, they listened as he went into a lengthy explanation of something called demyelination and how it could be "indicative" of one thing or another. He went on with a number of different medical terms, all of which were absorbed with limited understanding by the husband and wife. The word "sclerosis" came up, along with the term "multiple," and a realization took shape, at least to some extent. The husband interrupted the doctor to ask a question. "Are you saying that my wife has multiple sclerosis?"

The doctor went on about indications and other attributes, so he interrupted once again and asked the same question. The answer came back: "Yes, everything indicates that she has multiple sclerosis." Some additional conversation took place and the call finally ended.

The couple stared at each other, and then looked around at the same beautiful scene they had enjoyed a few minutes earlier. The breeze still smelled sweet and their baby was still laughing and bouncing. The late evening sun still shined and everything seemed exactly the same, but in those few minutes everything had changed ... or had it?

The future became uncertain, but is it ever truly certain? Indeed, it never is. And that became a Travel Forward moment for this young family. They could sit around and lament the diagnosis and what might happen, or **they could focus on living their lives.**

That's exactly what happened. Two years later, they invited another child into the world and they haven't looked back yet. In 2013, 16 years after the diagnosis, they continue to live their lives fully, with a focus on each and every day.

That couple is Mark and Karen Murphy. And yes, I happen to be that husband. ▥

TRAVEL FORWARD

Zen Buddhists say that there is no future, only the present. They have a good point, since the beauty of everyday experience—each moment—can easily go unrecognized when you're wrapped up in what happened at the office or thinking about what may or may not happen to you tomorrow, the next day, the next week or the next year. Each moment is precious.

Create a **DAILY "MOMENTS" CALENDAR OR JOURNAL** in which you write down the beautiful moments of each day. Of course, in order to do that, you have to practice mindfulness—seeing what's in front of you with gratitude for all that you have, and love for those close to you. Even seemingly mundane things, like making a meal, washing the dishes afterward or making the bed, can be exercises in mindfulness. Pay attention to your breathing during these moments. Practice this today, tomorrow and the next day, thinking about all of the good things you have NOW!

Now share these ideas with **#TravelForward** and be inspired by what your fellow travelers have written.

DAILY MOMENTS

1

2

3

McCartney and the Open Window

What do you want today, and how much will you pay for it?

The constant desire to acquire new possessions and experiences motivates many of us. We dream of the new house, the latest car, the expensive wristwatch, the cutting-edge entertainment system, the sublime vacation home or the cool tech gadget.

Take fashion, for example. There is always the latest style, which changes constantly. Every year, the industry's most respected innovators work on their new looks, and then release them with a huge splash on the runways of Milan, Paris and New York. The goal, of course, is to get everyone to update their wardrobes while fattening the wallets of those very designers and their retailers around the world. The annual release of the new, must-have acquisition is a great strategy. It's paid off for decades in the fashion industry, and in other businesses as well.

Or how about the beach house on Nantucket or St. Barts? Sounds pretty nice, though it may set you back a bundle.

Clothes, cars, phones or homes … all of this stuff can be great fun, generating that rush of excitement every time we get a new toy, pay big bucks for a "lifetime experience" or own something that we know broadcasts our personal esthetic, sense of good taste and general coolness. Life becomes an ongoing quest for something

"

Enjoy the little things, for one day you may look back and realize they were the BIG things."

—Robert Brault

new, shiny and sensational. Hey, all it takes is a bank account and a credit card, right?

One consumer, who hit it big early and often, is **Paul McCartney.** He has never wanted for anything based on his early success, a career that could have carried him for the rest of his life on royalties alone. And he didn't stop when he became financially independent or even after he earned fortunes many times over. His passion for music and the evolving landscape of listeners spread his talents to multiple generations, who still listen to him today.

If anyone in music could have anything in life, and I mean anything, it's Paul McCartney. He is wealthy beyond belief.

When you think about his success and all that it brings him, you might wonder exactly what his favorite things in life might be. You might expect him to say, "Taking my jet to a private island in the Caribbean" or "Flying to Paris for lunch ..." Whatever he wants, he can have, since money is never a concern.

In fact, Sir Paul has remarked about one of his very favorite things in life, and what he said may surprise you. He said that he loves to simply lie on his bed in the dark with the window open on a mild summer evening, feeling the caressing breeze as it flutters in. This is from a man who can have anything that money can buy and is adored by tens of millions of fans. He's sampled more than most of us will ever know in a lifetime, yet he can find appreciation in a simple pleasure that is available to us all—for free.

Think about the times that you've just sat back and taken in your surroundings. You've felt it, too. That wonderful sensation when your senses are alive, and your mind and body are in tune with the world around you. A calm comes over you, and your breathing becomes slow and rhythmic. You find an inner peace that is fleeting at times but, at that particular moment, fulfills you. You think, "This is where I belong right now ..." and you are right.

Life is full of such momentary gifts: the summer breeze, the rustling of leaves and the pure, loving gaze of a child. They're around us and available multiple times every day, and they just need to be noticed. They cost nothing yet are priceless.

Many of us go through life in a quest for possessions that we think will satisfy our inner souls, when that satisfaction can be met by simple pleasures that are always nearby: walking in a park with a childhood friend, sitting on a bench and watching the limbs on the trees move in unison to a light breeze or, like Sir Paul, simply lying on your bed and looking up at the ceiling.

When we feel our best, and when we are at our best, we appreciate the world around us. Paul McCartney has found gratitude in the most basic aspect of living. It could be his age, but more likely his outlook on life has brought him to recognize that the simple things are the most valuable.

We are only here for a short period of time—a fact that we all recognize as we age. There are only so many springs or summers left in front of us, so it's important that we take the time to appreciate each moment. ■

TRAVEL FORWARD

Begin now. Make a list of the simple things that you can do and experience every day for great pleasure. I'll start the list for you.

1. Witnessing a beautiful sunset or sunrise
2. Cuddling in bed with a loved one
3. Breathing the fresh air immediately following a thundershower
4. Watching children play with joy and innocence
5. Enjoying a pleasurable aroma that invokes a special memory
6.
7.
8.
9.
10.
11.
12.

Now start paying attention and seeing how many of these things you can appreciate today. How about tomorrow? This week?

SPREAD THE JOY.
Share your simple pleasures with **#TravelForward.**

> **"All that is important is this one moment in movement. Make the moment important, vital, and worth living. Do not let it slip away unnoticed and unused."**
>
> —Martha Graham

Appreciate Each Moment

Do you ever find yourself so busy in the moment that you never take the time to stop and simply appreciate what's there, right now, in front of you? A young baseball player, who made it to the top of the game, never appreciated those moments—that is, until it was too late.

Mike Robbins was living out the same dream that millions of children have when they are growing up. It usually starts when they are in Little League. They envision themselves as major leaguers, playing for their hometown team and looking up at a stadium filled with tens of thousands of screaming fans. Every kid who has ever swung a bat or thrown a ball has had that same dream.

"**You must live in the present, launch yourself on every wave, find your eternity in each moment."**

—Henry David Thoreau

It goes pretty much like this: The score is tied, and you come up to bat in the bottom of the ninth inning during the final game of the World Series. You take a few swings to loosen up, and then step into the batter's box to face the pitcher. The outcome of the entire season has come down to you, the pitcher and a ball that will travel towards you at more than 90 miles per hour. You are unfazed, and your focus has never been greater.

You fight off pitch after pitch and force a full count. The next pitch will either put you on base or end the game. The pitcher winds up, throws with all of his might and "crack" goes your bat. You haven't just made contact; you've crushed a solo homer over the fence, giving the team you grew up with the world championship!

A variation of this fantasy is repeated in backyards, sand lots and even on city streets all across our country. Sometimes you're the pitcher who shuts down the batter by striking him out, leaving his team with a one-run victory and the championship; at other times, you're the kid in the outfield who runs down the fly ball, climbs the fence and makes the spectacular catch to end the game.

It doesn't matter how it happens; it just does, and it's repeated over and over throughout our youth. Go ahead and think back to those days, and a smile will cross your face as you remember how you won a fantasy championship or two!

When most of us get to adulthood, we are running so fast that we never allow our fantasies, or our realities, a chance to play out. That happens to be the story of Mike Robbins, who pitched in the College World Series for Stanford and played three seasons in the Kansas City Royals system before sustaining a career-ending injury to his throwing arm. When Mike thinks back on his shortened career, he doesn't dwell on "what might have been," or how he performed, but rather what he missed during the time he played—specifically about not taking the time to "appreciate the moment."

"My one regret has had nothing to do with any of the games that I had lost or mistakes I'd made on the field—it was just that I didn't fully appreciate it while it was happening," he has said.

Mike's book, *Focus on the Good Stuff,* helps us appreciate what we have at any given moment. It speaks to the power of focusing on the positive and what we want, not what we don't have. He takes issue with the "culture of complaining" that has replaced an "attitude of gratitude" as a way of living your life.

Mike never pitched in the major leagues or won a World Series game, but he did get a taste of success—and later an appreciation—of what that could mean in his life.

Mike regretted his inability to appreciate the moment, but you don't have to suffer the same fate. Learn from Mike about what's really important as you journey through life. Make sure to fully experience and appreciate those fleeting moments. They make you who you are. ▥

TRAVEL FORWARD

It's so easy to be caught up in the events of the past or anticipate the future, missing the precious moments of your life as they occur. With a little practice, however, you can learn to live more in the moment.

No doubt you have looked at **family photos** from years ago and remembered fondly the moments when they were taken, whether they were precious times when your children were very young or other times with a boyfriend or girlfriend, your parents or dear friends. Why not freeze those moments as they're occurring?

Back to the Future

The next time you see a memorable or sentimental scene unfolding in front of you—one that you know you'll always remember—pause before you snap that photo and think of how, years from now, you will be staring at the image and remembering the beauty of the scene. Well, **you're there right now!** Pause a few extra seconds, breathe in deeply, think of nothing else but what you are witnessing and feel the joy of being in that moment, right now. It will never come again, but the beauty you feel now will last forever. Drink it in.

Record the first five moments like this that you experience over the next few days.

1 ....

....

....

2 ....

....

....

3 ....

....

....

4 ....

....

....

5 ....

....

....

The Gratitude Journal

Start a gratitude journal. Buy a small notebook and, throughout the day, write down things for which you're grateful. Try to enter at least five things each day. Create your own online gratitude journal and share the link with your fellow travelers with **#TravelForward.**

"If the only prayer you said in your whole life was 'thank you,' that would suffice."

–Meister Eckhart

Saying Thank You

Eckhart von Hochheim, known as Meister Eckhart, was a German theologian, philosopher and mystic who lived from 1260 to 1327. He was known for his ability to communicate the metaphorical content of the gospels to both laymen and clergy alike. It's this ability that makes his statement about saying "thank you" in the form of a prayer so profound.

These two words can take on a variety of meanings, depending on the context in which they are used in any given situation. Most of us use these words to acknowledge an act by an individual. It could be a waiter pouring a glass of water, a doorman helping you out of a car or a clerk handing you back some change from a purchase.

When it comes to personal encounters, where you are providing the act or are on the receiving end of someone else's kind act, saying "thank you" is both simple yet meaningful.

That's because giving thanks is a powerful tool that puts you in balance with people and the world around you. The gesture of holding open a door for the next person coming through is balanced by the appreciation shown by the words "thank you" from the passerby. It's a mutual moment where both feel that energy, that connection—even for a second, when they both Travel Forward.

"You're Welcome!"

"You're welcome" is another simple set of words that, when said with meaning, can change the dynamics of any interaction. By doing something for someone, we are giving of ourselves, even if it is a small gesture. When that action is recognized, we make sure we tell them that they are welcome. We are happy to make that gesture or do that task, and would gladly do it for them again and again. We acknowledge that we get something out of the interaction, even if we are the ones giving.

Small gestures that are recognized by others make us all stronger. In most cases, they don't require much in the way of effort or thought. Indeed, passing through a door and holding it for the next traveler adds nothing to the task. Slowing down your car to make space for the person in front of you doesn't alter your final destination or your time to get there.

What these simple acts do alter is our mindset as we go about our daily lives and how we feel about life and the people around us. Picture New York City, with sidewalks full of people who seem hell bent on getting somewhere fast. The determination on their faces is hard to miss as everyone, other than tourists from out of town, seems to be on some kind of mission. Nothing short of an earthquake can get these folks to move off their path on their way to whatever is next on their calendar.

Consider this scenario:

You head belowground to board a subway in New York City. There you are, hard-pressed to see someone make eye contact with another or do much else in the way of interaction. It's as if everyone is in their own little silo, oblivious to what's going on around them.

But everything in the subway car where you are standing is about to change. You watch an older woman board the train. She's moving slowly and making her way into the crowd of straphangers (a term that reflects the sheer fact that there are limited seats and most people are left standing during rush hour). Everyone watches as a young man stands up from his seat to offer this older woman's tired legs a respite. She whispers a word of thanks as she settles into her seat. He smiles and replies, "You're welcome."

The moment is profoundly activated and recognized, even on that crowded subway. It is the moment where the two of them, and everyone within range, felt something that was both simple and magical. It was a Travel Forward moment. ◾

TRAVEL FORWARD

Who do you know or admire who would be inspired by this story?

List:

- ◆ Their names
- ◆ Why they would be inspired (their personality traits)
- ◆ How many of these traits you share with them
- ◆ Traits or skills they have that you would like to acquire

Name a few moments you have experienced that have **positively changed the entire dynamic** of the social setting in which they occurred.

1

2

3

Now share them with **#TravelForward.**

Be a Johnny Appleseed of humanity. Practice the art of changing dynamics by consciously smiling at strangers and saying "please" and "thank you" in settings that could use a little boost.

Daily Reflections

You find yourself standing in front of a pond on a quiet day where the air is completely still and nothing seems to be moving. Your toes have ventured into the edge of the water, but the ripples they made have since spread beyond the eyes' view. You tilt your head down and look for the small minnows that are typically found in these ponds; instead, you see the reflection of your face and body as the sun above you, coupled with the water below, creates a gigantic mirror.

> **"Sometimes you find yourself in the middle of nowhere, and sometimes in the middle of nowhere, you find yourself."—Unknown**

You're startled because you didn't expect your towering figure and face to be staring back at you from the waters below, but indeed they are. What brought you here is lost momentarily as you take in your surroundings and put yourself at the center of it all. It's time to reflect.

Your face stares back at you, and it almost seems foreign. "Is that really me?" you ask. "Who am I, and where am I going?"

"Life can only be understood backwards; but it must be lived forwards."

—Søren Kierkegaard

Whether you are staring into a pond or a mirror, you need to take time to reflect on your entire being. **Understanding others begins with understanding ourselves.** Only through reflection can one begin this lifelong process that leads to self-improvement and fulfillment.

In a book that's about traveling forward, what can be gained by looking backwards? By looking backwards, you give yourself the opportunity to show gratitude for all that life has offered you. The good things in your life are here today but may not be here tomorrow. They are a blessing in time that can change in an instant, as the future can never be certain.

Just as these positive events can be fleeting, so will the negatives when put into the proper perspective. Did you have a bad day at work? Follow the Zen Habits and be thankful that you have work. Feeling overwhelmed by the demands of daily life? Be thankful that you aren't bored, for boredom can become the thief that steals your motivation and ambition.

An exercise in daily reflection and an acknowledgment to all that is good—and not so good—are powerful tools in moving your life forward. By understanding your past, you liberate yourself to change as you Travel Forward. ∎

TRAVEL FORWARD

No pond nearby? Look in the mirror. Look at yourself fully clothed, then take off all of your clothes and contemplate your body some more. What do you think are your best and worst features? What do these feelings say about how you view yourself overall as a person? Do they impact your behavior?

Take out a piece of paper and a pencil and pen—or even crayons! Draw a picture of whatever is on your mind, and don't worry about the level of your artistic talent. Just draw, giving form to whatever happens to be on your mind, such as a place you would like to visit.

DO IT NOW.

When you're finished, study the image that you created. What feelings does it reveal? What does it say about **you?** Consider your picture as a reflection of where you are at this moment. Dig deep. Does it reveal anything that you may not have considered before? What lessons can you take from it?

Create a list of 10 words or phrases that best describe you.

1 ....
2 ....
3 ....
4 ....
5 ....

6 ....
7 ....
8 ....
9 ....
10 ....

Now ask a close friend to make the same list about you. Compare the lists. What do they tell you about yourself?

Write a letter to yourself in order to explore feelings and present life. Then, immediately put that letter away for five days. After that period, pull it out again and (you guessed it) analyze it. Do you think it's honest? Uplifting? Depressing? Inspiring? Loving? What does it tell you about yourself?

What have you learned overall from these exercises? How might they impact the way you approach the world around you? Share your thoughts with **#TravelForward.**

Lifetime of Learning

" All the world is my school and all of humanity is my teacher."

—**George Whitman**

"How old would you be if you didn't know how old you are?"

—Satchel Paige

Attitude vs. Age

A young girl in her 20s struggles to find herself. She watches others around her as they seemingly advance their careers, build on their relationships and enter new phases of their lives. She is anxious and concerned that she's slipping behind in the race called "life." In a word, she feels LOST.

Even though she has yet to see the age of 30, she already feels old. She has always been considered beautiful and has never worried about her ability to attract a potential mate, but her concern grows daily. Part of that concern is the evidence around her. She sees younger girls and realizes that beauty on the outside is never permanent. She meets a new man, wills herself to fall in love and then becomes disillusioned when his thoughts and intentions are as deep as a kiddie pool. Despite the shallow waters, this woman could use a lifeguard as she finds herself being pulled underwater by a feeling of helplessness.

The feelings persist and intensify as she contemplates what her future might be, combined with the fear that she's realized it too late. She's suffering from what many refer to as a "midlife crisis" at the tender age of 28. She is struck by her belief that life is on some type of schedule—not unlike a school, where you move forward or get left behind.

Early on, she seemingly had the whole world in front of her. She dreamt big and imagined a fairy-tale life. She had envisioned herself in a successful career, with the man of her dreams, and thought that she'd have plans in place to start a family. She was raised with the belief that this was the path on which she was meant to be. Indeed, it seemed that her family and friends were following that exact same path, as she continued to move in one direction and then another.

"What went so wrong?" she pondered.

The answer is, "Nothing went wrong." Unfortunately, many can't seem to grasp this reality of life and living. **There is no preordained path to success in life.** Life is a series of events, meant to be experienced for what they are. Too many times, we view these events as stepping stones to something else instead of simply enjoying each moment.

When was the last time you simply stopped and stared at life around you? Instead of rushing to cross a busy street just ahead of the light changing, take a deep breath and watch everyone else around you. Do this in New York City, and you'll see people staring with awe at the buildings that surround them. Many are tourists visiting the city. Contrast their looks with the look of those who are on a mission—typically locals—to get somewhere. What would happen if you tapped one of those locals on the shoulder and pointed out a sign or a building? Chances are they would be surprised at what you see, for they have passed there a hundred times but have been largely blind to their surroundings.

What do you see when you look in the mirror? Is it the years of wisdom that are behind those eyes or is it something else? For this woman, it was the perception that the world was passing her by, even though she had barely begun living it. She was young, in the prime of life, but felt old beyond her years.

Here's what I would say to her: Life is not about age or accomplishments at any given time. It is about attitude. **What type of attitude do you bring to each morning,** when God gives you a chance to experience all that life has to offer? Do you look backwards and lament all that could have been, or do you eagerly look towards all that you are about to accomplish? Most importantly, do you appreciate the "now"? How well we achieve those attitudinal milestones in life is a better measure of success than all of that other stuff.

"No matter what age you are, or what your circumstances might be, you are special, and you still have something unique to offer. Your life, because of who you are, has meaning."

—**Barbara De Angelis**

A hundred years ago, life expectancy was the late 40s; if you made it to 50, you were beating the odds. Today, it's pushing 80 and moving higher, as medical breakthroughs extend both our lives and their quality.

Living longer provides more experiences and interactions by which you move your life forward—attitudinally! Celebrate your age, and manifest how the experiences you accumulate can help you Travel Forward, bringing those around you along for the exciting ride. ■

TRAVEL FORWARD

Name three people whom you most admire (they can be famous or just "regular folks"), and describe what it is about them that makes them so admirable. Do you share any of their admirable traits?

	Person	Why they're admirable	Like me?
1			☐
2			☐
3			☐

The admirable traits that you don't yet have can become your life goals. What can you do to work on achieving those traits, beginning today?

Get more in touch with your goals using these **daily practices:**

- **Recognize your gifts:** Think about the simple, good things that you are lucky to have in your life, such as health, comfort, food, the love of family or other good tidings. Think about these as you breathe inward deeply. Then, exhale and feel the joy. Resolve to live every day with mindfulness of these gifts. In periodic intervals throughout the day, practice this conscious breathing as you do.

- **Don't sweat the small stuff:** When everyday frustrations or worries about some future event get you down, remember that it's all "small stuff" compared to those gifts you have been given. In fact, read *Don't Sweat the Small Stuff—and it's all small stuff* by Richard Carlson.

- **Notice the beauty around you:** Be mindful. Look around. Enjoy the beauty of a summer breeze, a beautiful picture, some inspirational music or the myriad other things you encounter each and every day. Take that energy and pass it on to others.

- **Practice kindness:** When you're kind to others, you spread positive energy in the world, and you're always repaid with the joy and satisfaction that this attitude brings! Practice smiling at people who serve you in business, in stores and in your everyday life.

Do you have an attitude? Do you have the right attitude? Share your thoughts with **#TravelForward.**

"

It took me four years to paint like Raphael, but a lifetime to paint like a child."

—Pablo Picasso

When I Grow Up

When I grow up I'm going to ...

be an astronaut

be a princess

be a fireman

play in the NBA

be a scientist

design buildings

write a book

become an actor

live in a faraway land

... When I grow up ... When I grow up ... When I grow up ...

What's the big hurry?

What would life be like if we never grew up? Where could your imagination take you in your lifelong adventures if you saw the world as a child?

Everyone has dreams as a kid and an imagination that knows no limits. What did you dream about or imagine as a child while playing in your backyard or even in your room? Did you conjure up incredible scenarios and put yourself at the center of all of the action?

A few sheets and a couple of chairs, and suddenly you have built a massive fort that's hiding in plain sight. You are all but invisible to your sworn enemies just beyond your gates.

You've gathered your comrades, mostly stuffed animals, and have arranged them inside the fort. You look at them and nod your head in approval. They stare back at you as you determine how, together, you will conquer the world. Your Nerf gun is fully loaded, and you sneak a peak outside the walls of this fort, taking in the person who fed you breakfast but who is now your sworn enemy. Without making a sound, you take aim, fire and duck back inside.

You know that your shot has hit its mark as you hear an unintelligible squeal come out of your mother's mouth. *Bingo!*

Your mom is only too eager to play along with your fantasy as she staggers and lowers herself to the ground. You risk a look outside to confirm that you have indeed taken out the enemy. She's down and not moving. You slowly rise and make your way across the battlefield to make sure, only to squeal yourself as she quickly rolls over to her stomach and launches towards you.

You retreat to the fort where you know that you'll be safe from any approaching attack. "Phew, that was close," you think as you giggle nervously.

Your imagination is a powerful tool that can move you forward in life. Kids do it every day, as they lose themselves in fairy tales and games, played by themselves or with others. In their worlds, they are the center of the universe—something that will change as they mature and better understand the world around them. But the center of the universe also has a different meaning when it comes to kids. Each day, they create their own virtual worlds in which they plan, play, scheme and live life.

Imagination, curiosity and openness to new ideas—however fantastical or "outside the box"—are hallmarks of **approaching life with the eyes of a child.** As adults, we are told to leave behind our childish thoughts and ideas; in doing so, we are robbing ourselves of what brings joy and wonder to ourselves and those around us. With the eyes of a child, we can rekindle that joy as the ability to imagine the unseen—a new reality—and Travel Forward. ■

"Some day you will
be old enough to
start reading fairy
tales again."

-C.S. Lewis

TRAVEL FORWARD

Take yourself back to when you were a kid and **remember the games you played** and the things you did. Try to recall what a particular room was like ... or an entire house.

Look around the room you are in right now; if outside, take a look at what avails itself to you and your imagination. If you were eight years old again, how would you make the most of this moment? What do your eyes see now that they didn't see a moment ago? What are you drawn to? If you knew that nobody was watching, or judging, what would you do? Climb a tree? Jot down your thoughts below and share them with **#TravelForward.**

Rekindle Your Imagination Further

1. **Find a photograph** of a beautiful close-up scene from nature, and lose yourself in it. Where do you think it was taken? Can you picture the scene, the exact time and place, with the entire world going on around it? What happened immediately after the image was photographed? What happened to the subject? What did the photographer do? What is happening at that very scene this very moment? What story can you tell that begins with the photograph?

2. Now put on some **instrumental music** and assume a comfortable position, lying down or seated, in a place where you won't be bothered. If you're in a darkened space in the evening, that's even better. If you're listening with headphones or earbuds, better yet! Close your eyes, and let your mind be taken away by the music, but don't think about your actual life; instead, turn the music into an abstraction, a soundtrack of a completely original movie in your head.

When you finish with either of these exercises, **write a one-page story about what you fantasized.** Post it with #TravelForward.

Traveling Forward Through History

Do you really understand a particular situation, a people or an event? The only way to know this is to listen. Listening in and of itself provides a window into the world and the people around you, but there's far more to understanding than simply listening.

To truly grasp a particular moment or situation, you have to experience it.

Experiences come in many shapes and sizes. They are deeply personal and open our eyes and our minds, creating the first step to understanding. Travel provides the greatest opportunity to gather experiences. Many of these experiences will be individual in nature and unique to you; others will be a shared experience that hits you deeply in a way that is hard to fathom.

> To truly grasp a particular moment or situation, you have to experience it.

S tanding in a classroom, you hear no sounds other than the footsteps of a handful of others who are there with you, taking in the same surroundings. It's quietly disturbing as you stand, looking into the faces of hundreds of people, their black-and-white photos affixed to the rolling boards and the walls in the room. Maybe these rolling boards were once blackboards used to teach. Instead of pictures, they had words designed to motivate and inspire a generation of children.

Now, as you stand there, you are thinking of anything and everything but inspiration. You feel as if your body is sinking into quicksand and you can't get out. Your chest is heavy and it's difficult to breathe. You've never understood horror like this. Indeed, you've never experienced feelings like the ones you have at this very moment.

You are in the heart of Phnom Penh, and you have stepped into a nondescript former high school. Its days of teaching ended in 1975, but the education continues at what is now known as the Tuol Sleng Genocide Museum. The Khmer Rouge turned this high school into a prison camp from 1975 until 1979, torturing and killing up to 20,000 people during that period.

This atrocity took place while the world went about its business. Despite nightly news broadcasts and all types of reporting, millions were murdered in a civil war that sought the extermination of entire classes of people. It was a new holocaust that literally went unnoticed and uncovered by the media. Most of us find it difficult to grasp how something so horrific could take place. The cruelty and suffering seems hard to imagine but, standing here, it is all too real.

Other than through the movie *The Killing Fields*, most of us have never heard of these atrocities or paid scant attention to what took place. A classroom and a history book can provide an insight into what happened here, but written words can't convey the true horror. Only through travel can one live history, even decades or hundreds of years afterwards, bringing a particular moment to life.

Travel transports us physically but connects us mentally and emotionally to the world.

What can you learn about life and others when you travel? When it comes to Cambodia, no movie, book or lecture could convey what happened. Only through travel can you feel this experience at its core, and then Travel Forward as a result. ■

TRAVEL FORWARD

If you were to **pick five things**—places or areas of interest—that you would like to explore outside of your current life's endeavors, what would they be? Now place them in order of priority.

1 ....

....

2 ....

....

3 ....

....

4 ....

....

5 ....

....

Imagine how it would feel to learn and experience even a hint of all those things. Now just get started—even a tiny bit—with #1. You have a whole year to explore it.

Most news seems so negative. **Name three positive headlines** that have resonated with you in recent days.

1 ....

....

2 ....

....

3 ....

....

▶ Why did these affect you?

▶ What do they say about your values?

▶ What do they say about the type of people you admire?

▶ What do they say about your dreams?

Share your thoughts with #TravelForward.

"**Envy** is the art of counting, the other fellow's blessings instead of your own."

—**Harold Coffin**

Envy vs. Inspiration

The Hamptons: the summer playground of the rich and famous, and one where there is no lack of money on display. It seems, at times, that everyone who passes you by must be the owner of the latest dot-com success story or the old blue blood who inherited his wealth. What are you thinking as you view these endless displays of wealth?

Walking down the street on a beautiful summer afternoon is a 48-year-old man, who saves enough during the year to rent a small cottage for him and his two kids each summer. They can only afford a couple of weeks, but they look forward to these summer stays. They certainly can't rent anything near the beach, as those properties are dominated by the multimillion-dollar estates that can cost over $100,000 per month.

His name is Tom, and he's been coming here since he was a young man. He thinks back to those early days when he saw the amazing homes and the high-end automobiles, and dreamt of enjoying that lifestyle. Twenty-five years later, he finds himself at the height of his midlife crisis, which has him feeling bitter that his dreams have yet to be realized … and feeling, quite realistically, that they won't happen now.

Tom looks around and shakes his head, pinching his lips together in a bitter smile. He's not a happy guy as he wonders why it's them, and not him, who have made it

> *"Resentment is like drinking poison and waiting for the other person to die."*
>
> —Carrie Fisher

into this elite stratosphere of money, sports cars and designer clothes. Indeed, he grows a bit agitated as he continues his walk, and ducks into Starbucks where he can sip an overpriced latte—his one indulgence of the day. "They are no better than I am," Tom thinks, as tinges of envy and jealousy grow.

These feelings will stay with him for the rest of the day, and through most days, as he spends his hard-earned money on his only two weeks of vacation for the year. Later that day, when he drives back to his cottage and makes dinner for his boys, he'll tell them about these "rich" people and how they don't deserve what they have.

What are you thinking as you walk down the street and a Bentley passes you by? The driver looks young—indeed, very young. You immediately ascertain that he's not the driver for somebody else but is instead the owner of the car. What goes through your head at that moment? Are you impressed that someone so young is driving a car that costs in excess of $200,000? Do you think, "Well done," as that young man must have built something successful in order to afford such luxury?

Or are you immediately seized with envy, or do you have a feeling that somehow the person driving that beautiful car didn't quite earn it or doesn't deserve it?

What if this person made his riches on his own by starting a company and helping millions? Does that change your opinion for the better? What's your thought process when you hear that he is the son of a powerful Wall Street figure? Is your opinion any different?

In all of these scenarios, nothing has changed about the person in front of you. The only thing that has changed is your view of him: a view through the prism of your own lens, skewed by your personal biases and world experiences, not his. In the time that all of these observations took place, the person you are thinking about hasn't changed one bit.

Class envy and jealousy are two traits that have been with us for thousands of years. Since the time of Moses, we have heard, "Thou shalt not covet," but that doesn't seem to stop those feelings that so many of us have. What can we do about them as they trickle to the surface?

One of the most important things you can learn in life is how to free yourself from these kinds of destructive thoughts. Once you do, you can clear your mind and Travel Forward. ■

TRAVEL FORWARD

There are at least two big problems with holding envy for another person. The first is that your envy doesn't change the other person's status one iota. The second is that envy is self-destructive; it only wears you down and diminishes your own self-worth. Envy based on appearances of material possessions is especially bad, as the source of that envy may be totally groundless. **Covet what makes you unique.** Covet what you bring to those around you and help them Travel Forward with you.

Instead of wallowing in jealousy or envy, look for inspiration from those around you.

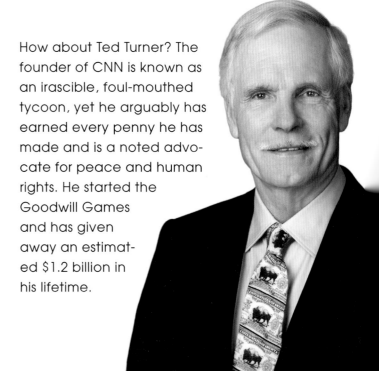

You may envy or despise this nerdy-looking guy, but the Gates Foundation has helped save the lives of more than 670,000 children in the developing world through its vaccination program.

How about Ted Turner? The founder of CNN is known as an irascible, foul-mouthed tycoon, yet he arguably has earned every penny he has made and is a noted advocate for peace and human rights. He started the Goodwill Games and has given away an estimated $1.2 billion in his lifetime.

What other wealthy people can you name who have brought gifts to the world? Share your thoughts with #TravelForward.

What positive traits make you unique? What could people learn from you? What can you bring to the world? List a few of your unique traits here.

1 ....

....

....

2 ....

....

....

3 ....

....

....

Discovering the Walk

On a group walk in the Amazon rainforest in Ecuador, a moment is frozen as the leader raises his right hand and everyone comes to an abrupt halt. Fausto slowly steps three feet off the path, leans down and picks up a tiny frog. The frog's body is no bigger than his thumbnail, yet Fausto is able to see this creature and catch it despite the leaves, the branches and everything else covering the jungle floor.

Fausto is completely tuned into his environment at that very moment. He's not considering his email account, what he's having for dinner, his monthly rent or anything other than the jungle. He has become one with his surroundings and has found one of its smallest creatures in the process.

"Live your life each day as you would climb a mountain. An occasional glance towards the summit keeps the goal in mind, but many beautiful scenes are to be observed from each new vantage point."

—Harold B. Melchart

This is not an ordinary frog, however. This creature has the ability to kill within an hour should its skin come in contact with an open cut, like the one on Fausto's hand. But Fausto not only finds the elusive frog, he comes away unscathed, since he profoundly understands the jungle and his own body. Everything is in sync.

Everyday life is likewise full of little discoveries and lessons. Nature and your external surroundings make for a world of fascination that can capture your imagination and take you to places far beyond your physical constraints.

You may look up on a walk and see an airplane trace across the sky, leaving a contrail in its wake. As you look closer, you may see a series of these same contrails, left by earlier flights, leaving paint strokes in the blue expanse. These are the paths taken by those who seek to explore new places.

What goes through your mind as you ponder the jet overhead?

Every time I see a plane, I feel a sense of awe. I've flown well over a million miles in my lifetime, and I still can't believe that we are able to rocket through the atmosphere in a round cylinder full of seats. Imagine 150 years ago, around the time of the Civil War, and what those people would think of a jet airplane cutting through the sky today.

My thoughts move from awe and amazement at the technological marvel that is flying to the passengers on board. Who are they and where are their travels taking them? Are they heading home from a long trip into the waiting arms of a loving family? Are they on the way to a strange land, filled with anticipation of what is yet to be discovered? Do they imagine the people they will meet and what those encounters might be like?

I think about these people and the many ways their lives will be affected by this trip. They are traveling forward on their own quests.

You don't need to travel to another part of the world in order to Travel Forward in your life. Indeed, you can take steps each day to Travel Forward without ever leaving your hometown. **It's about being in sync,** being aware of what's going on around you and slowing down just enough to make sure you don't miss it. ∎

"To be awake is to be alive."

—Henry David Thoreau

TRAVEL FORWARD

With what are you in sync?

What makes you completely at ease?

What do you notice around you?

Stop what you are doing and take a walk,

even if it's only around the outside of your house or apartment. Instead of going somewhere deliberate, have no destination in mind. Just observe. What do you see? Name three things that you see on this trek that you haven't noticed or stopped to notice before.

1 ....

2 ....

3 ....

Now write down two things to describe what you've discovered about each item.

1 ....

2 ....

Share your thoughts with **#TravelForward.**

Transcending "Fail"

What have you screwed up lately? How about last week, last month or last year? All of us have experienced one situation or another where we wish we could have a "do over." But why do we always want a do over? Why not just accept that particular failure and move on? If more of us did that, we'd grow and learn at an exponential pace. You're failing by not failing enough.

According to **Mark Twain,** "Good judgment comes from experience, but experience comes from bad judgment." Too many times, we strive for perfection; it's far more important for each of us to simply strive.

How many mistakes have you made on your way to gaining some insight into the worlds of business and relationships—heck, of the world we live in each and every day? Where have you exercised bad judgment, and what was the outcome?

My teenage son has used the word "fail" in my house over the past several years: "He failed." "Fail." "You failed." The kid just keeps pointing out people and events where there was a failure and, in his words sometimes, "EPIC FAILURE." It wasn't just him. It seemed that all of the boys he hangs out with speak the same language of failure. I didn't quite get the fascination with the running commentary in regards to people screwing up, and thought that these kids are pretty negative in their self-assessment as well as in their assessment of those around them.

A ride down the hill on a longboard ends with an arrested slide that has somehow gone awry, as these things typically do, and the kids scream out, "Failure!" A simple game of 21 on the basketball court gets the same review, when a foul shot that could have ended the game goes astray.

Over and over, kids are fascinated by the word "failure" and are quick to point it out, while adults are horrified by it. **As adults, we are looking for perfection in everything we do and in everyone around us.** Indeed, we are incredibly self-critical in many instances as a result of our mistakes. This assessment leads to a mindset that drives people to make even more mistakes. It becomes a self-fulfilling prophecy.

Negative Self-Talk

How many times have you disparaged yourself as a result of something you did or didn't do? Did you slap your head and say, "God, I'm an idiot," for forgetting some important date or activity? Or did you simply cry out, as I've been known to do, "That was so stuuuuuuuuuuupid"? People have a tendency to beat themselves up over mostly trivial things; when it is a bigger event or issue, they really start flirting with self-loathing.

What can be gained from all of this negative chatter? You might think nothing, but you'd be wrong. You do gain something, and it's not a good thing. It's called a "loss of confidence," which affects every aspect of your life. By filling your head with all of those negative thoughts and admonitions, you are digging yourself deeper and deeper into a dark hole. Keep doing it, and you eventually won't see any light; in fact, you begin to make those initially brief negative thoughts your permanent legacy.

What changes when you catch yourself doing something wrong, or even boneheaded, and then turn around and admonish yourself in the process? Does the event that took place change? Did you suddenly go back in time and reverse whatever happened? Nothing changes except the view of YOU, from the inside out, which then goes on display to the world around you.

What changes when your outlook goes from negative to positive? Usually, good things happen. Think about it.

If you call yourself a loser, you'll act like one. If you stay relentlessly positive, you'll Travel Forward. The path you choose will make all the difference in your life. ■

TRAVEL FORWARD

Starting today, tell yourself that **you will not allow negative self-talk** to enter your mind or pass through your lips. Use these statements as your mantra (filling in a few of your own).

"I will focus on what's ahead of me and not a negative event that's in the past."

"I will write down a series of positive affirmations and read them each day."

"I am a gifted person."

"I am unique in my talents and abilities."

"I am ....

"I am ....

"I am ....

Share your thoughts about this with **#TravelForward.**

SELF-DETERMINATION

4

> " I, not events, have the power to make me happy or unhappy today. I can choose which it shall be. Yesterday is dead, tomorrow hasn't arrived yet. I have just one day, today, and I'm going to be happy in it." **—Groucho Marx**

"It doesn't matter where you come from ... it matters where you are going."

–Condoleezza Rice

It Doesn't Matter Where You Came From

Where are you going? Are you focused on the past, the present or the future?

Too many of us feel limited by the past. We think about what we could have done differently in a certain situation or with a particular opportunity. We kick ourselves and fill our heads with negative, limiting thoughts. These thoughts become our personal governors, limiting us in our desire to take bold action.

Take a moment and think about these questions: What did you think about over the past 24 hours? Were those thoughts positive and empowering, or were they anchored in the past and limiting?

Did they look to the future, or keep you tied to the past?

"If only"

 "If only I were smarter ..."

"If only I were better looking ..."

"If only I had paid more attention in school ..."

"If only I had taken that job more seriously ..."

"If only ..."

"If only ..."

"If only ..."

Say this to yourself: "If only for the next few minutes, I will picture where I'd like to be in the next few years. I will take deep, cleansing breaths, and let my mind take a blank canvas and begin to paint that reality. As I become more in tune with my body, through my breathing, I'll feel the negative thoughts of the past melt away and a new future will emerge."

The first brush strokes will start and the picture will take shape. Envision what that painting will look like. What will the colors be? Will it be a setting that you know and love, and one that has special meaning, such as a sunset, a sunrise, a small boat bobbing in the sea or a majestic mountain?

Whatever it is, make it your own. See yourself in it, but remember one key distinction: You are more than the picture itself. You are the artist painting it, and it can be whatever you imagine.

Condoleezza Rice's parents painted a picture for what she could be, regardless of her circumstances. The power of that picture never left her mind, and she has achievements at the highest level. She was blessed to have parents who knew how to inspire her, but you don't need a specific person in your family to be able to feel and act on that inspiration.

She shared her personal story in a speech at the 2012 Republican National Convention, where she explained what it was like to grow up in the Jim Crow south. Her parents told her that, even though she might not be able to go into certain stores or restaurants, she could go on to become the President of the United States. Condoleezza's parents understood what it meant to Travel Forward and the opportunities that were available for their young daughter. Did she become president? She didn't, but she did become one of the most powerful women in the world when she assumed the office of the Secretary of State.

There are many stories like Condoleezza Rice's where, regardless of background or upbringing, people go on to greatness. Sometimes it's the influence of a parent, as in Rice's case, or the internal motivation to simply Travel Forward.

They are the first-generation immigrants, who came to the United States with hopes and dreams for a better life, and then created one.

They are the second-generation immigrants, who became the first members of their family to go to college.

They are the young athletes, who go out every day and give it their all. Even though they may not play above their high school team level, their dedication forges an attitude and a confidence that will take them higher and further in life than what anyone may have thought possible.

Traveling Forward is about not being limited by your past or by someone else's definition of who you are. It's about doing your best, whatever that level is. ■

TRAVEL FORWARD

Condoleezza Rice has shown us all what we can accomplish if we **just believe in ourselves**—if we cast off the self-doubt and the preconceptions of others to shape our own future. What other people can you name who have risen above their circumstances to achieve great success?

Famous People

	Name	Where they started in life	What they acheived
1			
2			
3			

People I Know

	Name	Where they started in life	What they acheived
1			
2			
3			

Now take just a minute to think about the traits that all of these people have in common. Contribute your thoughts on this with **#TravelForward** and you may be in my next book!

The Ultimate Late Bloomer

Most people in their 70s aren't thinking about what their next career is going to be. Indeed, some are trying to remember where they left their bottle of Maalox or when their next doctor's appointment is scheduled. Over the past 50+ years, we've been conditioned to believe that we should be "retired" and living some type of "golden-years" lifestyle.

What exactly does that mean to you?

Some will tell you that they are too old, even at 50, to consider taking up something new. Is it fear, or something else, that keeps them from taking the leap?

Anna Mary Robertson didn't have anything holding her back. Indeed, she was going to do something, even though she was already in her 70s. You may not know her by that name, but you probably know this one: **Grandma Moses.** This woman wasn't going to simply stop at some magical age that the rest of the world called "retirement." It didn't matter what birthday she had reached; she was going to do something new with her life.

"If I didn't start painting, I would have raised chickens," she said.

And paint she did. She didn't attend any kind of art school or take one of those art courses you see advertised. She just started putting oil on canvas, pressed

121

wood, Masonite—you name the medium—using her memories of the past and what was before her at that moment. In doing so, she created evocative images of rural life.

"What a strange thing is memory, and hope; one looks backward, the other forward; one is of today, the other of tomorrow," she opined. "Memory is history recorded in our brain, memory is a painter; it paints pictures of the past and of the day."

Grandma Moses didn't set out to become famous or make any money. She simply painted, and quite prolifically at that. During her three decades of painting, she produced over 1,600 pieces. Her early paintings sold for $2 or $3, depending on the size … and often there were different renditions of the same subject. Money was not her motivation, and her talent wouldn't be denied. In 2006, more than 40 years after her death at age 101, one of her paintings sold for $1.2 million.

We've been conditioned to believe that we need some kind of programmed training in order to become competent or capable in any chosen field, but is that really true? Some, like Grandma Moses, discover an inner ability that just needs to be nurtured to grow. Others simply need to be able to disconnect from their currently hectic lives and free their minds for the endless possibilities that are present. Either of these scenarios might come at a point in our lives where most people have literally "checked out."

At the age of 88, *Mademoiselle magazine* named Grandma Moses a "Young Woman of the Year."

At the age of 88, *Mademoiselle* magazine named Grandma Moses a "Young Woman of the Year."

Most people don't go outside of the boundaries that they've set for themselves or that others have seemingly imposed on them. They are either afraid to try, afraid to fail, or maybe both. When it comes to outside influences, they begin to believe the naysayers and start to take third-party opinions, based on someone's own limiting beliefs, as fact. A fear of the unknown creeps in and, if left unchallenged, keeps that person from realizing what could be a very rewarding move.

The only way we grow is by challenging ourselves to go beyond our own self-imposed limits.

Living a full life is about experiences, and doing new things creates those experiences. There's nothing to stop anyone, at any age, from realizing his or her dreams. Ignore the outside world, zero in on what you are passionate about, and understand that anything is possible.

If you have doubts, all you have to do is think of this 70-something grandmother, who followed her passion and became an American icon! ■

The only way we grow is by challenging ourselves to go beyond our own self-imposed limits.

TRAVEL FORWARD

Who says that you can't change careers or do anything you want at any point in life? Think about your situation now. **Are you really doing what you love?** If not, WHY not? It may be time to leave your comfort zone. It may be a little scary at first, but the reward in happiness could be huge! Figure out what's been holding you back, confirm your talent or skill in this area (formal training is not required) and then resolve to take the first step forward, however small.

What I would really love to do.

Why I might be good at this.

The first small step!

Contribute your thoughts on this with **#TravelForward.**

You Choose How Good You Want to Be

I was running a little ahead for an appointment just outside of Manhattan and found myself dropping into Drago Shoe Shine at the Port Authority—the bus depot on the west side of Manhattan and the best spot to park a car. The exit ramp for the Port Authority puts you right into the mouth of the Lincoln Tunnel, without having to touch a city street. This can be a big advantage when you're in a hurry to get out of town, as I typically am.

With a few extra minutes to spare, I sought out the second-floor shoeshine spot and grabbed a seat. I wanted to make sure that I looked my best for an afternoon appointment across the river in Hoboken.

I expected a quick shine, for which these New York establishments are so well known, leaving me plenty of time to make my 1:30 meeting. For anyone who has ever been to New York and taken a few minutes to get a shine, they'd understand that these guys are both fast and efficient. They get you in and out, doing as many shoes as possible in any given day. But today would be different than any of my other shine experiences, counted in the hundreds.

I took my spot in Lenny's chair. He's a man who turns a shoeshine into an entertaining piece of art, with the canvas being the leather on your feet. He gazed at my shoes and told me how we were going to approach the pebble finish in a way that would "amaze my eyes." Amaze he did, and not just with the finished product.

After sizing up my shoes, so to speak, he got to work, but it didn't seem like work. Lenny was bouncing from one side of the chair to the other, as he put his brushes and rags to work. This was accompanied by a running conversation about shoes and his 45 years in the business.

I'm not one to sit with the newspaper when I have an energized and engaging person in front of me, so I was carrying on a conversation with this highly entertaining individual. When I walked up, I had commented on how he had been eating something and he told me that he's always eating—something that the two of us immediately had in common. I eat between six and eight different snacks and meals throughout the day, which keeps my metabolism running so high. It seemed like this approach was having the same effect on Lenny, as he didn't appear to have an ounce of fat on his body. Indeed, I immediately handed him the nickname "Fat Man Johnson," and politely asked his colleagues to make sure it stuck.

But I digress. This is a story about what drives people to greatness in any particular area, and the pride that goes along with that accomplishment. As we jibbed and jabbed back and forth, and as Lenny did his dance as if in time with the conversation, he pointed to an article from *The New York Times,* which was affixed to a plaque. It featured an interview with the man before me, dishing on his view of the world from the ground up, literally.

He then said something that stopped me in my tracks: **"You choose how good you want to be."** It was a Travel Forward moment. I asked him to repeat what he had just said, and he kind of looked at me funny, as if to say, "I didn't say anything remarkable …," but indeed he had. In fact, he said something that everybody, in every walk of life, should take to heart, but one that many never do.

YOU CHOOSE how good **YOU WANT** to be.

You choose how good you want to be. YOU CHOOSE how good YOU WANT to be. In life, in love, in business and in any endeavor or relationship, it's up to you how you will tackle it. Can it be that simple, some may ask? Others might cast this off as being naïve, or unrealistic, but they'd be wrong. There are many things that are outside of one's control, but choosing to be the best in your particular area isn't one of them. Even though Lenny's approach was simple and straightforward, it really was quite profound to see it in action. ■

TRAVEL FORWARD

Think about the people whom you come across day after day in various roles: the lady at the checkout counter, the gardener, the barista, the lawyer and the street sweeper. **They all choose how good they want to be.** Some choose excellence.

Name three people with whom you have crossed paths lately and who are worthy of your own "Good as You Can Be" Award, and describe HOW you know that they have chosen to strive for that level of personal quality.

	Who they are	How they show it
1		
2		
3		

Now choose JUST ONE activity of your own where you could reflect your "Good as You Can Be" esthetic. JUST ONE! Write it here.

Contribute your thoughts on this, AND a photo of you doing it, with **#TravelForward** and see what others are doing along the same lines!

THIS IS JUST STEP ONE! Master one activity, and then try another!

Self-Esteem and the Trophy Mentality

In an effort to build self-esteem with our youth, some people who are involved in sports are destroying it. I call this the "Trophy Mentality," where everybody, on every team, gets one. They don't get the plastic statues for winning the championship or some other great feat. They get it for just showing up and playing the game. *Really?*

We all know the saying, "Half the battle is showing up," and may have used it on occasion; however, if you make that the benchmark for the success of your child, you are setting them up to fail. How can we ever expect our children to Travel Forward in life when they are told that simply showing up is worthy of some kind of special reward or recognition?

Imagine a Little League baseball game consisting of fifth graders. Little Joey steps up to the plate and misses nearly every pitch thrown his way—a pattern that continues for the entire season. Indeed, there is barely a hit in any given game, as his entire team struggles with each at bat. The parents in the stands complain incessantly that the umpire has it in for their fifth-grade boys, to be known heretofore as the "Hapless Hitters." They yell from the stands, **"Are you blind, ump?"** and "You couldn't see a ball if it hit you in the head!" And that's just in the first two innings of the game. This marathon of overhyped adults and the Hapless Hitters will continue for the next two hours; indeed, it will continue all season.

The kids in the dugout aren't deaf; they are listening to the boisterous complaints from the stands and forming their own opinions. The first thing they conclude is that their performance isn't about them; it's about the umpires. They don't feel that it's their fault if they have not honed their baseball skills. The blame has been laid at someone else's feet. Their parents are making sure that they blame the ump, the coach and even some extraterrestrial event for their child's lack of ability. Certainly, it couldn't be that baseball just isn't their thing!

Not everyone is going to be good at baseball, sports, academic endeavors or any number of other activities. Unfortunately, however, many are brought up to expect, and even demand, some kind of level playing field when it comes to life in general. The world is afraid to make anybody feel "bad," so instead we have gone in the opposite direction by telling everyone that they are great.

This mentality creates a vacuum that can't be filled by deeds and accomplishments, as many are simply unable to live up to the false narrative of their youth. Instead of a feeling that they are traveling forward in life, they come to the conclusion that they are never quite what they thought, if they ever reach that point of self-awareness. Most don't.

Too many children are being raised to believe that they are special beyond how God made them. Everyone has a special gift to bring to the world, but that can take many forms and may not be in the areas of sports, business or performing. What happens when someone comes to the realization, later in life, that they are not quite what they were built up to be by others? Will they shake that feeling off and get back on track? Will they become disillusioned, or worse, when they discover that being exceptional isn't bestowed on you by others but instead is something you build yourself?

It's important for us to believe in ourselves and not in some narrative that's imposed upon us. We all have the ability to excel in our chosen area, but we need the ability to find that path at some point in our lives.

It comes down to what makes us unique and what we can do to discover our gifts. Effusive and undeserved praise and rewards in our youth lead many to conclude that they are something they aren't, robbing them of the ability to discover their true talents.

Developing your true talents involves passion. The key is finding yours and living it. ∎

TRAVEL FORWARD

How do we teach our children, or even ourselves, to find and **develop passion?** What's an alternative to "undeserved praise"? Maybe a place to start is to think of what you enjoy doing when you have the option of doing anything.

What do you enjoy doing the most?

What makes this enjoyable?

About what are you passionate?

Name something that you are good at and enjoy doing. Are you doing it enough? Why or why not?

Name something that you are not particularly good at but enjoy doing. How can you develop this skill?

Name something that interests you that you haven't tried before. What's stopping you from trying it?

Contribute your thoughts on this with **#TravelForward** and see who else shares your interests!

"Vision without **action** is daydream. **Action** without vision is nightmare."

—Japanese proverb

Taking Action

Have you ever walked past a storefront or read a magazine article that featured a new product, and thought, "That was my idea!" Indeed, many have felt that strange sense that comes with seeing a previously pondered concept brought to life by someone else.

Ideas begin in your head and, for most people, that's where they end. There is no lack of ideas, for they are all around us. We are innately creative in seeing things, based on our experiences, which others might not have recognized just yet. But how many of us capitalize on those recognitions?

The homemaker, who struggles to open a jar, searches for and finds a seemingly unrelated item. She uses it to grip the lid and finds it turning easily in her hand. She makes a note of it for future reference and goes about her day. Two years later, as she's watching late-night television, she sees a commercial for a "new" jar opener that "is easy on your hands and on your wallet ..." She shakes her head as she tells herself, "Darn, I already thought of that!" This new product was simply a manufactured version of what she had used herself: a flat piece of rubber that assisted in gripping the top of the jar and getting it to move. She wasn't the first person to use this technique, or the last, so what happened? *Someone* happened.

While everyone else went back to their day-to-day world, one person stepped up and did some research into what he or she thought was a potentially novel product. That person did what I'm encouraging you to do: He or she took action. Despite the long odds to create something unique and profitable, there's always someone out there who seemingly defies those hurdles and their self-doubt and makes it happen. Why can't that be you?

What separates the super successful person from the masses is the ability to take an idea and execute it.

That execution begins with action. It begins with those first few steps, or one very bold step, to get things moving. However, it doesn't begin *until* that first step is taken, which requires commitment to the idea and the long road ahead to bring it to reality.

> **"Many great ideas go unexecuted, and many great executioners are without ideas. One without the other is worthless."—Tim Blixseth**

Can you do it? If you think you can't, it will never happen; if you think you can, it just might. There are no guarantees that you'll turn your idea into a successful product or business, but you'll never know unless you finally commit to making it happen. Remarkable products and services don't just occur spontaneously. They come from people who are quite ordinary in the beginning and end up extraordinary in time.

When starting out in business, I always was amazed at the people ahead of me in their careers, as if they had some unique talent that had magically put them into that role. Whether it was a media executive, a talented speaker or a writer, I looked at them, and then at myself, and thought, "I have a long way to go ..." Over the years, I discovered that they weren't any different than I was per se but just further along their chosen path.

I focused on the things that made them successful, set up a plan to emulate that success and then took action. It came down to a belief in myself and in my ability to evolve and grow over time. My career path became a series of steps in a long journey, where I could enjoy the experiences and learn from my successful colleagues along the way. **Each step I took allowed me to Travel Forward.**

Take action, one step at a time, and Travel Forward in your life. You can do it! ∎

"People become really quite remarkable when they start thinking that they can do things. When they believe in themselves they have the first secret of success."

—Norman Vincent Peale

TRAVEL FORWARD

Spend this week paying attention to things that you do often in your everyday life, and think of how they could be improved with some kind of **innovation or invention.** You'll be surprised at how many things you think of if you just keep this task foremost in your mind. Write your ideas here as they occur.

I wish I had one of these...

	Innovation/Invention	What it would do
1		
2		
3		

Do some research. Create a list of inventors who had ideas and acted on them, and then became hugely successful. List here the three most inspirational people for you, and describe what you have in common with each of them.

These folks inspire me

	Who	How we're alike (My Success Factor)
1		
2		
3		

Now take the first step. Commit to developing one of the ideas in your first list, using **My Success Factor** identified in the second list. Keep track of your weekly progress here.

Week # / What I Achieved

Week	Achievement
1	
2	
3	
4	
5	
6	
7	

Oneness

" We can only be said to be alive in those moments when our hearts are conscious of our treasures."

—Thornton Wilder

"

One of the
main points about
travelling is to
develop in us
a feeling of solidarity,
of that oneness
without which
no better world
is possible."

—Ella Mailart

Truth at the Pyramids

A dream trip to experience one of the great Wonders of the World—the Pyramids of Giza—is put on hold for fear of personal attacks that could lead to injury, or worse, death. That, I assumed, is Egypt today.

Who in their right mind would travel to this ancient land at a time of upheaval not seen in decades? The images are burned into your brain from every medium.

But time changes things. You might consider going, only to again feel doubt the moment you turn on your television and witness angry mobs that are seeming to gather all over the country. You recognize the central point of these protests, and the flashpoint for violence, as Tahrir Square. You also learn another, more ominous name to describe Tahrir Square: Martyr's Square.

You immediately conclude that the entire country of Egypt is on fire and only a fool would venture there. You make the decision that any planned trip to explore this cradle of civilization will take a backseat to the daily violence that's portrayed on screen.

Your eyes see the horror—and your brain flashes the warning, "STAY AWAY!" But no official State Department advisory is necessary to keep you from going there, as you've

"Breathe next to me. And I will capture a piece of your soul along with mine."

—Marikit dR. Camba

already determined that being the recipient of a stray rock to the head is not your idea of a vacation.

The world is a big place and Egypt is completely out of control. The thought of going there fills you with fear and trepidation. You are concerned that you could easily become a victim in a land where life appears to be valued at a different, and much lower, level.

I ventured to Egypt during this period, and heard the reminders from family and friends as to the mortal dangers I would be facing. I was implored to not go as the country appeared to be completely unstable.

As I set off from London to Cairo, I thought about what I might encounter on the ground. Would things be as chaotic as they appeared on television? What would people say to me and my crew as we ventured out to shoot video on location? What kind of security would be necessary to protect us from these crazy mobs?

It was late morning, and we had arrived at Giza to shoot some video at the pyramids. Tourism was down to almost nothing, and the Bedouin's camels rested on the hot desert sand as barely a western face could be seen. I strode around the base of one of the pyramids, walking towards what appeared to be an extended family having a picnic. Two men jumped up and shouted, "Hello! Hello!" My western appearance stood out and, for some reason, they wanted to talk.

As it turned out, these people were experiencing the pyramids for the first time, just like me, and they were excited to share their experience, and their family, with a perfect stranger.

Imagine what was going through my mind at that very moment. You move from a period of uncertainty, prior to embarking on this adventure, and then you remain a bit cautious once you arrive, only to experience warmth and acceptance.

Cut back to the media reports and you'd expect to see rocks flying, Molotov cocktails or worse. Instead, I experienced a slightly different projectile: a six-month-old baby in a pink fleece outfit.

Within moments of greeting me, a small bundle of joy was offered. **This family wanted me to hold their little baby!** Despite all of the red flags raised by the media, the only danger that I faced at that moment was from a burp gone awry, or perhaps some dribble. I found myself standing in a foreign land that had seen too much unrest, holding this foreign baby and cooing into its ear. It was both magical and eye opening.

It was a Travel Forward moment if there ever was one. In that moment, every perception that had been painted about Egyptians washed away. **The people of Egypt, in that microcosm of interaction, became one with me.** We shared the same hopes, the same dreams and the same incredible experience, as we stared at an ancient wonder experienced by millions of people who had come and gone before us. ■

"One Love! One Heart! Let's get together and feel all right."
—Bob Marley

TRAVEL FORWARD

You don't have to travel to Egypt to share my experience. **You can practice and develop your own "one-world" understanding every day of the week.** When you're at the mall, downtown, or just walking around your neighborhood, keep your eyes open and really observe the people around you. Some may look just like your family members; others may not. Watch them and think about how the dynamics of their friends and families mirror yours. Ponder what connects you with them, not the opposite. No matter where you go in the world—near or far—you can see this and think about the love and aspirations we all share.

Share the love. There is a Facebook page called "Israel Loves Iran," where people from Israel, Iran and any other place can post sentiments of mutual understanding and oneness, despite the threatening relationship between those countries and their leaders. The reality is that a mother in Tehran is not that different from one in Tel Aviv or Dallas. A Chicago father, who is busting his butt to provide for his kids, has plenty in common with his counterpart in Kabul, Nairobi or Jakarta. The political world is a chaotic place, with vested interests constantly competing, threatening and warring, and the international media largely plays along, painting nations in stark black and white.

Look for examples of international understanding online. List three that you've found and describe why they have moved you.

1 ....
....
....
....

2 ....
....
....
....

3 ....
....
....
....

LET'S TRY TO FIX WHAT'S WRONG.

What kind of social media, event or program do you think might help foster a sense of oneness among people of the world? Share your thoughts with **#TravelForward.**

"

Never believe that a few caring people can't change the world. For indeed, that's all who ever have."

—Margaret Mead

Africa Mercy

Four hundred and fifty crew members call it home. They also call it a lifeline to impoverished patients on the west coast of Africa, who are suffering and dying from diseases that are completely preventable. Its name is the **Africa Mercy** (www.mercyships.org)—the largest nongovernment-backed floating hospital in the world. It is completely staffed by volunteers, including 15 doctors, 90 nurses, technicians and ship crew.

Doctor Gary Parker came to the ship with the intention of staying on board for four months. As of this writing, it's been 26 years, and he has no intention of leaving. What drives a trained doctor, an expert in his field, to forego the trappings of wealth available to him and give himself to this cause? Most of us couldn't fathom this kind of sacrifice, and that's what makes Doctor Parker and the others on the ship so remarkable.

The idea started in 1978. Don Stevens started a charity called Mercy Ships and sought out volunteers who would staff medical ships and bring much-needed care to Third World ports. These volunteers didn't get paid then or today; indeed, they cover their costs to reach the ship on which they are working, and receive no compensation in the process. Some have spent the better parts of their adult lives on board, marrying and raising families. This is their life, and they wouldn't have it any other way.

As we look at their lives, we might marvel at the sacrifices they make by not being home, but those on board would quickly correct our perception. Indeed, many have stated that the rewarding nature of their work is more than any monetary reward. Others will claim that it gives them the ability to "see the world" and do it for free. All I can tell you is that more than 500,000 patients have been seen over the years, the impact of which is nearly impossible to quantify. Their sacrifice (although those on board would correct me and say their privilege) has impacted well over a hundred thousand people, who would have suffered in the shadows without them.

For perspective, you can simply look at what a five-month stay in a single port can reap: **281 patients**, some close to death, have benign tumors removed; 34 children have their cleft palates fixed; 794 patients, some who couldn't see for decades, have their eyesight restored. Miracle? No. It is just a collection of committed individuals, who have come together to enhance the lives of their fellow man, woman and child.

If we spoke to the many people helped by this collective, you might get a different take, with a miracle being part of that discussion. Imagine being blind for 10, 20 or 30 years, and then suddenly being able to see again. Imagine that this transition takes place in a matter of a day or two, when the cataract that covered their lens is removed and a new lens is put in place. You wouldn't hear an argument that this is indeed a miracle for that individual.

Miracles do happen when people come together around a particular cause. When that cause brings a group to a foreign land, one not understood by those who

"The only limit to your impact is your imagination and commitment."

—Tony Robbins

have never traveled, another miracle takes place. That miracle relates to the common humanity that runs through all of us and is tied to an awareness of what we are all like as individuals.

Some aboard Africa Mercy might be college-educated and board-certified doctors, while others have no education other than what they have learned from their tribes. It doesn't matter. They are drawn together by the power of travel and by the desire of one to help the other Travel Forward in life.

They benefit from the greatest gift of all: the ability to see the impact of their actions, and the life-changing effect they have on those they touch. ∎

TRAVEL FORWARD

You can make a huge difference in the lives of others, whether you do it off the coast of a distant continent or right in your community. If you've got desire and dedication, and a concern for others, then you're already on your way. Consider the following:

What is the **greatest challenge** you ever have faced?

....

What was the result? Did you meet the challenge?

....

What talents and inner resources did you call upon to address this challenge?

....

Using **#TravelForward** describe the biggest challenge you've ever faced and compare your experience with those of your other Travel Forward compadres. What traits do you think you have in common with them? What traits do you think you could develop in order to be more successful in facing future challenges?

What is one potentially useful trait that you think you could develop in order to help people in need? Try to employ that one talent on small tasks over the next 24 hours, and keep it in mind as you go about your day. What positive difference did it make in your day and in the lives of others?

Share your thoughts with **#TravelForward.**

Everyone Craves It

She was born during China's Cultural Revolution, when capitalists and educated citizens were placed into "re-education" camps in the countryside. Mao Zedong's China forced young city people to move to rural areas where they could "learn" from the peasants. This ideological mission caused a great deal of economic and social disruption at the time. Despite this, a woman named **Zhang Xin** would find her way. It was a circuitous route that took her from adolescence in the Chinese countryside, and then to two different continents as a young adult, only to end up back in China.

Her mother brought her to Hong Kong when she was 14. There, she would work during the day on a factory floor while attending school at night. This would continue until she was 20 and had the means to buy a wok and a one-way ticket to London. Indeed, she knew that she'd have little opportunity to eat out and wanted to be prepared to make her own meals. As she ventured to a land where the people "looked strange"—she had never seen so many Caucasians in her life—she found her way to a job at Goldman Sachs, the venerable banking firm. **This is a true rags-to-riches** story that would be remarkable had she stayed at Goldman Sachs and continued her odyssey on Wall Street, but that was not to be.

After getting her start in high finance, she went back to China. Today, she's the fifth richest woman in the world and is reported to be worth $4 billion.

What's remarkable about Zhang Xin's rise is how it began in a China that denounced capitalism but became possible because of a China that celebrates it today, albeit in a measured way.

In a *60 Minutes* interview that aired in 2013, Zhang Xin discussed how her country was being liberalized through real estate. She recounted the story of her future husband, who took her to a construction site that contained what she described as the "largest hole I'd ever seen" in the ground. He told her at that time that "this is the place that will be the Manhattan of Beijing." She

> ## "The secret of happiness is freedom. The secret of freedom is courage."
> ## —Thucydides

laughed as she recounted it, explaining that he had never been to Manhattan, so how would he have an idea of what the Manhattan of Beijing should be? The video cut to large structures as Lesley Stahl, the *60 Minutes* correspondent, stated, "It's not Manhattan ... it's bigger!"

Despite all of her success, Zhang Xin still understands the many challenges that China has to face. She knows that it's still not the "Land of the Free," and shares her perspective in her interview:

"I hear a lot in the U.S. people praise Wall Street; people praise ... state capitalism in China look at how efficient things get done, decisions get made so quick and so effective it can roll over a policy overnight nationwide ... here in the U.S. we need to go through Congress, Senate and debate. ..."

But she's quick to point out that, despite the growth and all the business success in China, something has been missing.

It comes down to something everyone around the world craves: freedom. People need it and want it, and China will

"For Chinese living in China ... Chinese ... if you ask one thing everyone craves for is what? It's not food, it's not home, everyone craves for democracy—8,000 miles away people in China are looking at it (America); longing for it."

157

ultimately have it. As more and more Mainland Chinese acquire wealth, and with it the ability to travel, they will experience a world that Zhang saw as a young woman.

They will absorb those experiences, and many will bring them back to their homeland, just as Zhang Xin has. China will be far better for those experiences, as people who Travel Forward typically take others with them. This is the start of a movement that can change the lives of more than a billion Chinese people. ▪

TRAVEL FORWARD

When you **Travel Forward**, how can you bring people along with you?

1 ....

....

....

2 ....

....

....

3 ....

....

....

Watch Zhang Xin's *60 Minutes* **interview.**

Share your thoughts with **#TravelForward.**

"I think there's just one kind of folks. Folks."

—Harper Lee, *To Kill a Mockingbird*

People to People: Cuba

Jay-Z and Beyoncé, with their vast wealth and resources, can travel anywhere in the world at the drop of a hat. Access to private jets and all the trappings make it easy for them to literally just get up and go.

In early 2013 they did just that, jetting off to an island nation that the average American is banned from visiting: Cuba. This visit struck a nerve on all fronts, and especially with Cuban Americans, who have lobbied against lowering sanctions for Cuba. Decades of repression make it hard for these former refugees to understand why anybody should be allowed to enrich the dictators, who have held their family members and fellow countrymen hostage since the 1950s—a feeling that most of us can understand.

But instead of getting angry at their visit, you can view it through a different lens. When something like this happens in our celebrity-obsessed culture, the news outlets can't seem to get enough of it. That was indeed the case with this particular celebrity couple and their decision to travel to Cuba. This coverage brought a spotlight to Cuba and the issues that the Cuban people face. Those who protested the visit started to see the silver lining in the uproar it created: By putting Cuba at the top of the news cycle for several days, it put the plight of the Cuban people there as well.

Under a program known as **People to People** (www.peopletopeople.com), started by President Bill Clinton, Americans were given the opportunity to travel to Cuba if it was deemed educational in nature. That means the typical beach vacation, with mojitos and beer, wasn't going to be on the travel itinerary. Instead, travelers would have a full schedule that includes visits with locals and stops in an orphanage or two.

Eyes Wide Open

With two eyes and two ears, most of us can judge a situation and gain an insight. Those who travel to Cuba have the ability to understand the situation there and share that perspective with others. Many who originally traveled there were journalists, with platforms to influence others based on what they saw. This was extremely important, as they could amplify their voices across different media and put their spotlight on what they saw.

Today, every consumer has a platform to do something similar, albeit on a different level. It's called "social media," and it means that we can take a situation or an experience and broadcast it to the world. It might start with our circle of friends and family, but then take on a life of its own when those people decide to share it with their circle. This can continue until a single message, produced by an individual, can be seen by more people than the best-selling newspaper ever could in its prime. That's powerful.

People to People offers an educational program to visit Cuba today, even though it's technically illegal for Americans to travel there in general. It's also a way to describe how social media works. By opening up the opportunity to visit Cuba, even for Jay-Z and Beyoncé, and their not-quite educational trip, it allows that message to be spread from one person to the next.

For those interested in seeing change in Cuba, what could help more than this kind of exposure? From one person to the next, multiplied by the thousands, a movement takes shape and drives change. It is about people and how some of us can create a movement that, at its heart, defines what it can mean to Travel Forward.

One of the most amazing things about the power of travel is how it opens our eyes to other people and their culture. A celebrity couple and their unexpected trip to Cuba may have done more to help the American people understand this country's situation than any number of other efforts. In the end, if all of us Travel Forward as a result, isn't that the objective? ■

Acclaimed author Paul Theroux has written, **"Tourists don't know where they've been, travelers don't know where they're going."** He's got a point. True travel is about being surprised and learning something new about a place or a culture. Organizations, such as People to People or Next Step Travel (www.peacecorpsconnect.org/resources/next-step-travel), specialize in cultural exchange trips that can be magnitudes more fulfilling than conventional tours. Why not take one of these trips yourself? Find out more about these kinds of organizations and book your trip!

So ... where are you going to go?

The strangers who help or influence you while traveling become part of some of your strongest memories.

Perhaps you're lost in the street maze of Venice, only to be guided to the nearest osteria by an elderly woman, who then tells you her entire life story. Even in your own town, you may strike up a conversation with a stranger that turns around a lousy day or makes you reevaluate your life. List some of the memorable encounters you've had abroad and close to home, and describe what you took away from each experience.

Now share the best of these experiences with your compadres: **#TravelForward.**

"When I hear somebody sigh, 'Life is hard,' I am always tempted to ask, 'Compared to what?'"

—Sydney Harris

Images in Motion

Travel creates living reminders of how similar many of us are and how different our experiences can be. I was blessed to be born in the United States, into a middle-class family, and to have the opportunity to be educated. A blessing indeed, and one that I cherish as I explore various cultures and their respective challenges. When people lament their current situation or plight, they need to understand that there is always someone who or someplace that has a greater one.

This can be seen in a variety of ways. It could be a flight into the Amazon jungle in Ecuador, where landing on a dirt strip brings a collection of small, barefoot children who are quite curious as to what this single-engine plane may be bringing to their remote villages. Is it just a supply run, or are there people on board who will spark their curiosity about the outside world? For these residents, the world consists of their village, the surrounding jungle and the waterways that they traverse for their sustenance.

As I flew over the Amazon rainforest in one of those planes, all I could see was the jungle below and the twisting waterways. No sign of life was visible to the naked eye, yet a world of activity was taking place under our flight path. Most of that activity was confined to the animals that call the rainforest their home, but there were villages here and there where the people lived off the land. Most of the inhabitants had never watched a television or seen the modern world to which many of us are so accustomed. iPhones, computers, iPads and soaring skyscrapers would seem as foreign to them as a trip to Mars would feel to someone like me. Yet, they go about their lives and take what the land and their environment provide. They raise families, support their community, become grandparents and then pass on to their next life.

Halfway around the world, the experience is the exact opposite, as I transit one of the most congested cities in the world: Ho Chi Minh. This Vietnamese city, known to many as **Saigon,** is home to almost eight million people and is one of the most congested cities in the world. This congestion creates a constant energy that manifests itself on the streets and in the traffic.

Scooters are the main mode of transportation, and you see them everywhere. There are an estimated five million scooters on the city streets, and they are responsible for moving individuals, as well as families, to their next destination.

One evening, as my taxi slowly moved through traffic, I looked out the window to the right and saw a sea of scooters. Other than the sheer numbers, the one alongside my door stood out. A family of five was on the scooter, consisting of a father and a mother, two adolescents and a baby. The kids by my estimate were four, two and six months, respectively. Now, close your eyes and imagine that you are driving the scooter. Your two-year-old is sitting in front of you, your four-year-old is clinging to your wife's back at the end of the bike and your six-month-old baby is lying on her back across the seat between you and your wife. To the passing eye, you could almost miss the infant if not for the bottle being held in the woman's hand. **Yes, she is feeding her newborn infant on the back of the scooter,** as her husband and her two other kids navigate the streets of Ho Chi Minh City in evening rush hour.

You can see images like the one I captured in the Amazon and Vietnam through the videos we shoot and the pictures we take when we travel all over the world. With the millions of phones on the street, most with camera and video capabilities, and the various social media platforms, images of the world are easily accessible. What isn't so prevalent is the ability to immerse yourself in a particular locale to capture these images, as they are in motion before you.

There's nothing quite like being there in that moment, as images of life in different cultures manifest themselves right before your eyes. That can only be achieved via travel and the unique way it makes us think about our world and those with whom we share it. ∎

What fleeting moments have you experienced that have given you a brief but profound insight into the lives of others? Share your thoughts with #TravelForward.

Keep an Open Mind

We've all seen them: the guy muttering to himself on the sidewalk; the woman pushing the shopping cart full of clothing; a would-be Kobe Bryant, disheveled and in rags, shooting imaginary baskets as he weaves among pedestrians on the street corner; the crazy lady dancing in the street.

But wait a second ... are these folks really crazy? The way I see it, not every oddly behaving person is a mental case. Some just live outside of what we might call the "mainstream," and there are an infinite number of shades to humanity. So why do we lump people together? Why are we so quick to judge and categorize them?

I think it's laziness. After all, we live in a hyper-formatted society, where music, radio, television and people are given a label. You're told where to sit, what to like, what to fear, how to dress, what to listen to or watch, what slang to use and how to behave. Looking at someone for three seconds, and then consigning them to a prefab category, is the lazy way out.

On the other hand, what takes real effort—and maybe more than three seconds—is keeping an open mind and giving those whom you encounter a chance. Don't let others tell you what to feel and think. Expand your horizons and absorb more of the world. That wacky lady dancing around the intersection may be deliberately sending her joy your way, so why shut it out? Welcome eccentricity and encourage the improbable. It's the only way to Travel Forward. ■

Destinations Redux

At the beginning of the book, I asked you to jot down your thoughts about destinations and what they mean to you. I asked you to name both physical *and personal* destinations, noting why they were your favorites and why you found them compelling.

Now that you've traveled through this book, do you feel any different about these?

Go back and see if you would change or add any destinations. Have you already changed your path through life? That may be a good thing.

Keep a running list of physical and personal destinations that you hold dear. Keep them as a meditation and definition of who you are, and who you can become, as you Travel Forward!